A Guide
to the
Concise AACR2
1988 revision

---

a programmed introduction

Other titles by Eric Hunter published by Library Association Publishing Ltd

Cataloguing / Eric J. Hunter and K.G.B. Bakewell. —
3rd ed. / revised and expanded by Eric J. Hunter. —
1991. — 334 p. — ISBN 0-85157-467-X

Examples illustrating AACR2. —
2nd ed. — 1989. — 235 p. — Paper. —
ISBN 0-85365-649-5

An Introduction to AACR2 : a programmed
guide to the second edition of Anglo-American
cataloguing rules 1988 revision. —
1989. — 190 p. — ISBN 0-85157-457-2

A Guide to the
Concise AACR2
1988 Revision

---

a programmed introduction

Eric J Hunter
with the assistance of
Margaret E Graham

LIBRARY ASSOCIATION PUBLISHING
LONDON

© Library Association Publishing Ltd 1994

Published by
Library Association Publishing Ltd
7 Ridgmount Street
London WC1E 7AE

First published 1994

British Library Cataloguing in Publication Data
A catalogue record for this book is available from the British Library.

ISBN 1-85604-088-7

Typeset from author's disk in 11/13pt Times by Library Association Publishing Ltd
Printed and made in Great Britain by Bookcraft (Bath) Ltd

CONTENTS

Introduction 1

How to use this book 7

Special note on layout 7

Phase 1 Description (frames 1–41) 9
Phase 2 Choice of access points (frames 42–86) 33
Phase 3 Choice of access points – Added entries (frames 87–100) 57
Phase 4 Headings (frames 101–161) 65
Phase 5 Uniform titles (frames 162–172) 97
Phase 6 References (frames 173–189) 105
Phase 7 Analytical added entries (frames 190–195) 115
Phase 8 Worked examples (frames 196–210) 121

Appendix One   Illustrative examples 139

Index 145

ACKNOWLEDGEMENTS

The authors are grateful to the following publishers for permission to reproduce the material noted:

Chambers Harrap Publishers Ltd
> Title page and verso of title page from The German travelmate / compiled by Lexus, with Ingrid Schumacher. — New ed. — 1991;

Charly Records Limited
> Label and container inlay from sound disc Singin' the blues / Bix Beiderbecke. — 1993;

The Haworth Press, Inc
> Title page and cover from the first issue of the Journal of business and finance librarianship. — 1990-   ;

J. Arthur Dixon Ltd
> Postcard Wordsworth heritage / photography by Phil Insley. — [198-];

Library Association Publishing
> Title page from The basics of data management for information services / Peter G. Underwood and Richard J. Hartley. — 1993;

McGraw-Hill Book Company Europe
> Title page from Typing : first course / Archie Drummond, Anne Coles-Mogford, with Ida Scattergood. — 4th ed. — 1982.

INTRODUCTION

A *catalogue* is a list of, and index to, a collection or collections of books and/or other materials. It enables the user to discover:

> what material is present in the collection
> where this material may be found.

The second of these functions is usually performed by a classification number or some other means of location. The first function is covered by *descriptive* cataloguing, which is that part of the cataloguing process concerned with the description and identification of an item, as distinct from the determining and indexing of its subject content. Thus the term 'descriptive' relates not only to the way in which a particular item may be described but also the choice and form of headings under which it is to be entered. For example, here is a description of a book:

> Successful business computing / M. Tampoe. —
> London : Butterworth Scientific, 1982. — 124 p. : ill. ;
> 22 cm. — ISBN 0-418-01217-X

This description gives the catalogue user various pieces of information about the work: the title, the author, the publisher, the date, the number of pages, the fact that it is illustrated and the size, or height, in centimetres.

Headings under which this item would need to be entered would include the author, Tampoe, and the form which this heading will take would also have to be decided. Possibilities might be:

> M. Tampoe
> Tampoe, M.
> or   Tampoe, F.M.K.

The last name is given in the preface but not on the title page of the work.

Chosen headings are placed above the description to provide complete 'descriptive' catalogue entries, e.g.:

> Tampoe, M.
>   Successful business computing / M. Tampoe. —
> London : Butterworth Scientific, 1982. — 124 p. : ill. ;
> 22 cm. — ISBN 0-418-01217-X

A catalogue entry such as that shown here would be equally useful in a bibliography. The same principles are applied to the compilation of both catalogues and bibliographies.

The manner in which a catalogue entry is to be organized, with regard to which elements are to be presented, the order in which these elements are to be presented and the punctuation which will separate these elements, will be decided by a set of rules or cataloguing standard. This standard will also advise on choice and form of headings.

This text has been written in order to help the student gain an understanding of this process of descriptive cataloguing using a simplified version of the most recent and widely used international standard. This standard is *Anglo-American cataloguing rules Second edition 1988 revision* (*AACR2*) and the simplified version is *The concise AACR2 1988 revision* – hereinafter referred to as the *Concise AACR2*.

AACR2 is used throughout the English-speaking world, by the national libraries of Australia, Canada, Great Britain and the United States, and by other major English language cataloguing agencies such as the world's largest bibliographic utility OCLC, which serves over ten thousand participating libraries and has nearly 30 million records in its online union catalogue! *AACR2* has also been translated into a number of foreign languages such as Arabic, French, Japanese, Norwegian and Spanish.

The rules for description in *AACR2* are based upon the framework of ISBD(G) – the International Standard Bibliographic Description (General) – which was originally drawn up jointly by the Joint Steering Committee for the Revision of AACR and the IFLA International Office for UBC (IFLA = International Federation of Library Associations and Institutions; UBC = Universal Bibliographic Control). The rules can be applied to library materials of every kind. They provide guidance for the cataloguing of any item from a manuscript to a computer file, from a printed sheet to an oil painting.

Computerization has led to an ever increasing commitment to networks and shared cataloguing. Where the exchange of bibliographic records in machine-readable form is concerned, the best known communication format is MARC (MAchine Readable Cataloguing) format and MARC conforms to *AACR2*.

The *Concise AACR2* is designed to meet the needs of the many practitioners and students to whom the full text tells more than they need to know, or wish to hear, about standards and procedures for catalogue making. It also attempts to address the need expressed in third-world countries for a set of basic rules, stated in simple English, that could be used by relatively untrained personnel for relatively small and uncomplicated catalogues. It prescribes the same cataloguing practice as the full text, but restricts itself to only the more generally applicable aspects of that practice. The terminology is more 'user-friendly'. Reference should be made to the full text for guidance on problems not covered by the concise version or for a fuller explanation of some rules.

Cataloguing is not an exact science. The interpretation of cataloguing rules in certain instances may be open to debate and an individual point of view.

The rules may be considered in such cases to be guidelines or pointers in determining how a particular item may be described and the headings under which it will be entered.

When using the *Concise AACR2* the first step in the cataloguing of an item is to describe it. Questions must be answered such as 'What is its title?' 'Who is responsible for its content?' 'Who published it?' 'What is its physical format? etc. All of the elements which constitute the answers to these questions must be combined to form a standard descriptive format.

Having described the item, access points, or headings, under which the item is to be entered must be chosen. Access points may include the title, the responsible person or body, the series, etc. One of these access points is selected as the heading for the main entry, the complete catalogue record of an item, presented in a form by which the entity is to be uniformly identified and cited. Other entries then become added entries and the headings related to those entries are referred to as added entry headings. The *Concise AACR2* recognizes that some catalogues do not distinguish between main and added entries. If this is so then the rules are used to decide on all the access points to be added to a description and the distinction between main and added entries is ignored.

Having chosen the access points, or the headings for the main entry and for other added (i.e. secondary) entries, problems regarding the form that such headings may take must be resolved and references must be made from forms of heading which are not used but which may be sought by the catalogue user.

The processes which must be completed when using the *Concise AACR2* are illustrated in flowchart form in Figure 1.

To illustrate more clearly how the *Concise AACR2* may be used, let us consider some of the descriptive cataloguing problems posed by the work *Typing : first course,* the title page of which is reproduced on the facing page.

Problems:	*Answers provided in the Concise AACR2 by:*
1 How is the item to be described? For example, how are the title, the responsible persons, the edition, and the publication details to be recorded? In what order should these elements be presented and what punctuation should separate them?	Rules 0–11 The description of library materials
2 What access points are to be provided? For example, are there to be entries under the title and under all three authors?	Rules 21–29 Choice of access points
3 What forms of heading are to be used for the chosen access points? For example, is 'Coles-Mogford' to be entered under 'Coles' or 'Mogford'?	Rules 30–44 Headings for persons
4 What references are to be made from forms of heading not chosen? For example, if 'Coles-Mogford' is the form of heading chosen, should a reference be made from 'Mogford'?	Rules 62–65 References

Typing : first course will be referred to in various frames throughout this text and the solutions to the above problems will be given.

Typing
First Course
Fourth Edition

Archie Drummond,
Matthew Boulton Technical College, Birmingham

Anne Coles-Mogford,
Matthew Boulton Technical College, Birmingham

with

Ida Scattergood

McGraw-Hill Book Company (UK) Limited

London · New York · St Louis · San Francisco · Auckland · Bogotá · Guatemala · Hamburg · Johannesburg · Lisbon · Madrid · Mexico · Montreal · New Delhi · Panama · Paris · San Juan · São Paulo · Singapore · Sydney · Tokyo · Toronto

5

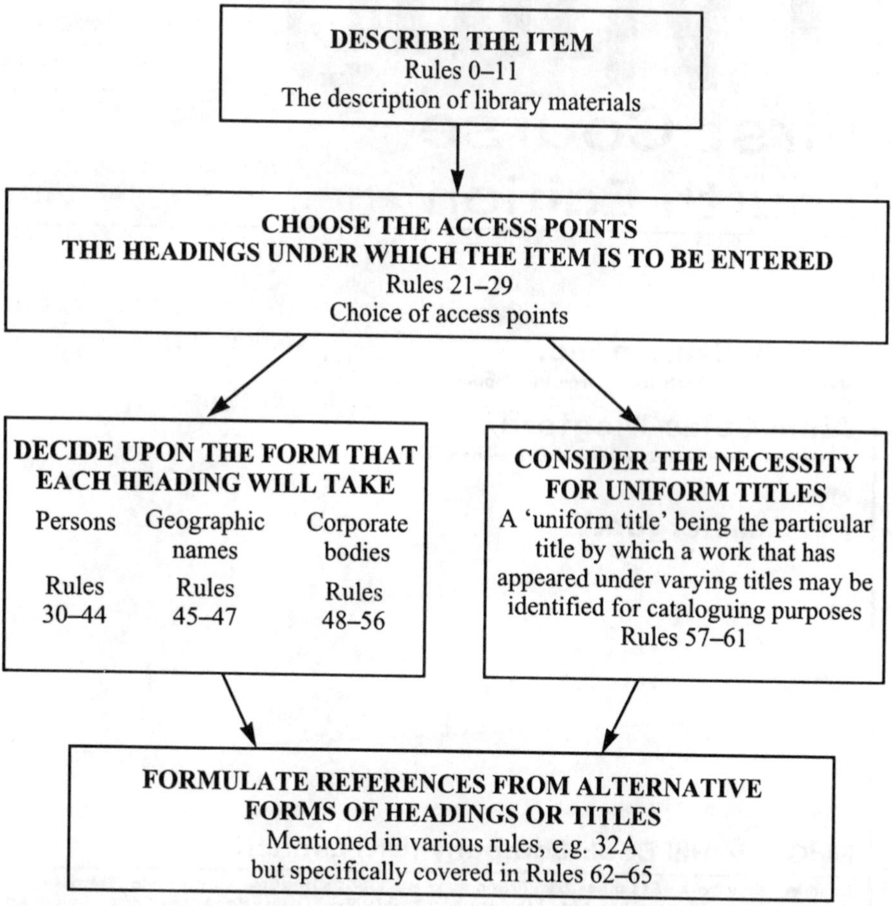

```
┌─────────────────────────────────────────┐
│           DESCRIBE THE ITEM              │
│              Rules 0–11                  │
│    The description of library materials  │
└─────────────────────────────────────────┘
                    │
                    ▼
┌─────────────────────────────────────────────────────────────┐
│              CHOOSE THE ACCESS POINTS                         │
│  THE HEADINGS UNDER WHICH THE ITEM IS TO BE ENTERED          │
│                  Rules 21–29                                  │
│               Choice of access points                        │
└─────────────────────────────────────────────────────────────┘
         │                                    │
         ▼                                    ▼
```

DECIDE UPON THE FORM THAT EACH HEADING WILL TAKE

Persons	Geographic names	Corporate bodies
Rules 30–44	Rules 45–47	Rules 48–56

CONSIDER THE NECESSITY FOR UNIFORM TITLES
A 'uniform title' being the particular title by which a work that has appeared under varying titles may be identified for cataloguing purposes
Rules 57–61

FORMULATE REFERENCES FROM ALTERNATIVE FORMS OF HEADINGS OR TITLES
Mentioned in various rules, e.g. 32A
but specifically covered in Rules 62–65

Fig. 1   Work flowchart for the Concise AACR2

HOW TO USE THIS BOOK

This programmed text is designed to teach the principles underlying the *Concise AACR2*, rather than a detailed knowledge of the rules themselves. The *Concise AACR2* is a cataloguing tool and, as such, it should be available for consultation as required. Rules should not be learned 'parrot fashion'. Therefore you will need a copy of the *Concise AACR2* by you as you work through the program. You should use it as directed and to help solve the set problems.

Lessons and problems are divided into *frames*. These are numbered for easy reference and they must be worked through as instructed.

The course as a whole is divided into a number of separate sections, or *phases*, as indicated on the contents page.

It may be necessary to refer to general reference books from time to time. Every cataloguer must have direct access to sources of information on a variety of topics.

Before turning to phase one and beginning this program, you should read the General Introduction to the *Concise AACR2* (pages 1–3).

SPECIAL NOTE ON LAYOUT

The layout of the descriptive element in sample catalogue entries included in this text follows that of the *Concise AACR2*. The *Concise AACR2* directs (page 2) that any heading added to the description is distinguished by placing it on a separate line above the description, e.g.:

> Brodie, Fawn M.
> The devil drives : a life of Sir Richard
> Burton / Fawn M. Brodie ...

No other instruction relating to the presentation of headings is provided.

In this present text, the heading is shown in bold type, e.g.:

> **Brodie, Fawn M.**
> The devil drives : a life of Sir Richard
> Burton / Fawn M. Brodie ...

This is done in order to make clear the difference between an access point chosen as a *basis for a heading* and the actual form that that heading will take. Thus:

Fawn M. Brodie

is the chosen access point and:

Brodie, Fawn M.

is the form that the actual heading will take.

Another chosen access point might be:

The Library Association

and:

Library Association

is the form that the actual heading will take.

In addition, certain parts of the heading are italicized. Thus, if the following name was chosen as a basis for a heading:

Baroness Orczy

the form that the heading would take when used as an example in the *Concise AACR2* (see page 97) is:

Orczy, Emmuska, Baroness

but this would appear in this present text as:

Orczy, Emmuska, *Baroness*

This indicates that, in this case, it was necessary to add the term *Baroness* to the heading.

This policy of using bold and italicised type in headings has been chosen deliberately in the hope that it will make explanations clearer to the reader. It is also, in fact, the way in which headings are shown in the full *AACR2*.

The word processor is now a common tool and typefaces such as bold and italic can easily be produced. In addition, the computer has enabled cataloguing agencies to produce variously formatted records from one machine-readable database. *AACR2* recognizes this and, thus, examples are illustrative and *not* prescriptive. Each library and cataloguing agency will need to develop its own 'in-house' style and its own in-house entry layout.

DESCRIPTION

Concise AACR2 Part 1

Part 1 of the *Concise AACR2* contains instructions on how to make a description of an item. *All* types of library material are dealt with concurrently.

Before proceeding to frame 1, read the Introduction to Part 1 of the *Concise AACR2* (pages 5–6).

FRAME 1

Every item to be catalogued must be described using a standard format. This means that each description must contain the *same basic components*. These must always be cited in the *same order* and be preceded by a *consistent punctuation*. Such standardization facilitates the local, national and international exchange of materials data and is particularly important in computerized systems. To a machine, '*David Copperfield*' and 'Charles Dickens' are simply strings of characters. The computer cannot identify one as the 'title' and the other as the 'author' *unless* it is 'told' which position in a descriptive record each will occupy and how each will be introduced.

Proceed to next frame.

FRAME 2

To achieve the standardization referred to in the previous frame, the description is divided into the following areas (see rule 0C), always cited in the order shown:

title and statement of responsibility	1
edition	2
special area (*only for* serials; computer files; maps, etc.; music)	3
publication, etc.	4
physical description	5
series	6
notes (a *repeatable* area)	7
standard number and terms of availability	8

It is not necessary for *all* of these areas to be present in every case. An item may not, for instance, be included in a series or have a standard number. Similarly, a note may not always be required.

The number given on the right is the relevant rule number for that particular area.

Proceed to next frame.

FRAME 3

The first frame referred to three major conditions which must be satisfied in order to achieve standardization of cataloguing descriptions. Can you remember what these conditions are?

Proceed to frame 31 for the answer.

FRAME 4

Each description must contain the same basic components and these must be cited in a consistent order. The basic descriptive areas were listed in frame 2. Each of these areas may be further subdivided into constituent elements, for example, the 'publication, etc.' area could contain elements such as the place of publication, publisher and date of publication (see rule 4).

Attempt to identify the major elements which together make up the 'physical description' area by referring to the appropriate rule in the *Concise AACR2* as given in frame 2.

Turn to frame 29 for the answer.

FRAME 5

With regard to the third condition for standardization, which is a designated, consistent punctuation, each area other than the first is introduced by a full stop, space, dash, space (. —). Alternatively, an area can begin a new paragraph (see rule 0D).

Elements within areas must also be divided by consistent punctuation. For example, a first statement of responsibility is always preceded by a space, diagonal slash, space (see rule 1A1), e.g.:

> A tale of two cities / Charles Dickens

What punctuation separates place of publication, publisher and date within the 'publication, etc.' area?

Turn to frame 40 for the answer.

FRAME 6

Information to be included in the description is extracted from 'prescribed' sources. For each of the common types of library material there is a chief source and information found in the chief source is to be preferred to information found elsewhere. The chief source of information for a book, for example, is the title page and, for a sound disc, the label or labels (see rule 0A).

If information cannot be found in the chief source then it is to be taken from:

      1) any other source that is part of the item;

or

      2) any source that accompanies the item and was issued by
         the publisher or issuer of that item (e.g. a container).

If all else fails, information can be taken from any available source (eg a reference work) or can be composed by the cataloguer.

If information has been taken from outside the item or has been composed by the cataloguer, it is enclosed in square brackets and the source is given in a note.

Find the chief sources of information for:

a) a map;
b) a computer file;
c) a serial.

Turn to frame 30 for the answer.

FRAME 7

One or more sources of information may also be prescribed for certain areas within the description. What sources of information may be used for obtaining the information to be included in the edition area?

Turn to frame 26 for the answer.

FRAME 8

As indicated in previous frames, the basic descriptive areas, with the required preceding punctuation, are as follows (see rule 0D):

      Title and statement of responsibility. — Edition. — Special
      area. — Publication, etc. — Physical description. — Series. —
      Note(s). —Standard number and terms of availability

Inserting the relevant basic constituent elements for a printed book into these areas, together with the required punctuation, would amend this layout to:

      Title / Statement of responsibility. — Edition. — Place
      of publication : Publisher, Date. — Pagination : Illustration ;
      Size (i.e. height in cm.) — (Series). — Note(s). — Standard
      number (viz. ISBN)

Substituting details relating to an actual item would give:

Modern mathematics at Ordinary Level / by L. Harwood Clarke. — 2nd ed. — London : Heinemann Educational, 1970. — 212 p. : ill. ; 23 cm. — (Heinemann's modern mathematics series). — With answers. — ISBN 0-435-50253-0

This is the basic descriptive layout for a printed book. Note that rule 0D allows for paragraphing to replace the 'full stop, space, dash, space' punctuation. Paragraphing is often utilized for the physical description area, for the notes area and for the standard number, e.g.:

Modern mathematics at Ordinary Level / by L. Harwood Clarke. — 2nd ed. — London : Heinemann Educational, 1970
212 p. : ill. ; 23 cm. — (Heinemann's modern mathematics series)
With answers
ISBN 0-435-50253-0

Whether paragraphing is adopted or not, and to what degree it is adopted, will depend upon the 'in-house' style of the particular library or cataloguing agency. As it is a variable option, paragraphing will not be used throughout the remainder of this text; layout will conform to the first of the examples given above.

Using this sample, basic layout, and without referring to the *Concise AACR2*, produce a description for the following item:

Small garden series

IMPROVING YOUR GARDEN
by
Oliver Dawson

London Pan

Revised edition
1972

ISBN 0 330 02896 0

The previous edition was published in 1967 by Collingridge of Feltham as *Making the most of your garden*. The book has 165 pages numbered in Arabic. It is illustrated and is 18 cm. high.

When you have completed this description, turn to frame 41.

FRAME 9

Basic layouts for other media, conforming as they must to the rules, are very similar to that for printed books, but obviously there will be differences in detail especially where physical description is concerned.

Here is an example:

> Keyboard fingering / Pictorial Charts Educational Trust. — London : P.C.E.T., [ca. 197-]. — 1 wall chart : col. ; 70 x 97 cm.

Compare this description with that of the printed book given in frame 8. Note that only the following areas are present in this instance:

> Title and statement of responsibility. — Publication, etc. — Physical description

Edition, series, notes and standard number areas were not required but they may well be required in descriptions relating to other wall charts.

The following description is for a serial:

> Home beer and winemaking. — Vol. 1, no. 1 (Jan. 1970)- . — Wirral : Foremost Press, 1970- . — v. : ill. ; 28 cm. — Monthly. — ISSN 0041-090X

As you can see, the description includes a title area, publication, etc. area, physical description area, a note (i.e. the frequency) and the standard number area (i.e. ISSN). A series area and a statement of responsibility (which is an element within the first area) are not needed in this example, although they may well be needed for other serials. Note particularly that, for a serial, use is made of the special area (see frame 2). In the case of a serial, this area consists of a designation (volume, part, number, etc.) and/or date of the first issue (see rule 3A), e.g.:

> Vol. 1, no. 1 (Jan. 1970)-

The designation could be numeric and/or alphabetic. Note that this designation/date should be followed by a hyphen and four spaces (rule 3A1). There are, additionally, other rules that apply specifically to serials. Rule 5B4, for example, relates to the extent of 'live' multipart items such as serials that are still being issued. In this case, for printed materials, 'v.' is used, preceded by three spaces. Rule 7B1 also relates, in part, to serials and makes provision for giving a note on the frequency.

Lastly, here is a description of a game (for which, in the context of the *Concise AACR2*, the appropriate term is 'three-dimensional object'). List the areas which are present in this description and those which are not.

> Kan-u-go : the crossword card game. — Leeds : Jarvis, Porter, 1934. — 1 game ; in box 8 x 12 x 2 cm. — For two to seven players and also Kan-u-go alone patience. — Instruction booklet (28 p.) in lid

Turn to frame 24 for the answer.

FRAME 10

The sample descriptions for various media considered in the previous frames have been included to provide some indication of the overall objectives of Part 1 of the *Concise AACR2*. Although such basic layouts are useful from this point of view, it must be appreciated that these are simple, illustrative examples. In practice, the cataloguer will encounter many hundreds of different, and sometimes very difficult, problems. Many of these problems will be covered by the *Concise AACR2*, but the user is referred to the full text for guidance on problems which are not dealt with (see page 1 of the *Concise AACR2*).

Here is an example of a common cataloguing problem. A publisher may well operate from more than one place and these places will be shown in the published item, e.g.:

HAMLYN

London New York Sydney Toronto

1974

Which of these places is to be included in the publication, etc. area? Guidance will be found in rule 4C2. Refer to this rule and decide what would be included in the publication area for this item by a cataloguing agency in Canada.

Turn to frame 32 for the answer.

FRAME 11

Problems relating to publication are not confined to printed books. Refer to rule 4 and attempt to discover what should be included in the publication area for a sound recording which bears on its label both the name of the publishing company (CBS Records of London) and also the brand name of the publisher (Epic), the latter being cited after CBS but in a more prominent position.

Turn to frame 35 for the answer.

FRAME 12

Having considered, in general terms, the contents of a description, the individual constituent areas will now be examined in more detail. This will provide an indication of the way in which the *Concise AACR2* approaches some of the everyday problems that may arise.

The first area is the 'title and statement of responsibility' area (see rule 1). A title is transcribed from an item exactly as to wording, order and spelling but not necessarily as to punctuation and capitalization (see rule 1B1 and, for capitalization, Appendix 1b of the *Concise AACR2*).

For example:

ORDER OF BATTLE OF BRITISH ARMIES IN FRANCE

would become:

Order of battle of British armies in France

The general capitalization rule for titles in the English language is that the first letter is capitalized but otherwise only lower case letters are used, except for the first letters of proper nouns and adjectives. Hence, in the above example, only the first letter 'O', the 'B' of British and the 'F' of France are capitalized.

A parallel title is preceded by a space, equals sign, space (see rules 1A1 and 1D), e.g.:

The barber of Seville = Il barbiere di Siviglia

Any additional unit of title information, for example, a subtitle, (see rule 1E1) is preceded by a space, colon, space (see rule 1A1), e.g.:

The fox, the hare and the rooster : a Russian folk tale

or   Typing : first course
(see reproduction of the chief source of information for this item on page 5)

If other title information is lengthy and does not contain important information it is omitted (rule 1E3).

If an item lacks the prescribed sources of information from which a title may be extracted, a title must be supplied from the rest of the item or elsewhere (eg a reference source). If no title can be found anywhere, then one is made up. A supplied or made-up title is enclosed in square brackets (see rule 1B6), e.g.:

[Wooden chair]

Now attempt to transcribe the following title:

OUT OF THE DINOSAURS
THE EVOLUTION OF THE NATIONAL LENDING
LIBRARY FOR SCIENCE AND TECHNOLOGY

Turn to frame 38 for the answer.

FRAME 13

Imagine that you are cataloguing a banana! What would the title statement be?
Turn to frame 36 for the answer.

FRAME 14

An optional inclusion, following the title proper, is a 'general material designation'. This consists of a term chosen from a supplied list enclosed within square brackets (see rule 1C), e.g.:

> Hamlet [motion picture]
> Hamlet [sound recording]
> Sir Winston Churchill [sound recording] : selected speeches

As this is an *optional* rule, it will not be used in the remainder of the examples in this text, but remember that the rule does exist if you want to use such material designations as 'early warnings' to the catalogue user.

In the full *AACR2*, there are two lists of general material designations, one for the use of British agencies and one for the use of agencies in Australia, Canada and the United States. The list in the *Concise AACR2* is the latter list (with the exception of the designation 'text', which is not used in the *Concise AACR2*). The list for use in the UK is much shorter with less specific designations in many instances, the argument being that these are *general* designations and that specific designations should appear in the physical description area. This is the UK list from the full *AACR2*:

> braille
> cartographic material
> computer file
> graphic
> manuscript
> microform
> motion picture
> multimedia
> music
> object
> sound recording
> videorecording

Proceed to next frame.

FRAME 15

The statement of responsibility which appears first in the chief source of information is always given, recorded in the form that it appears in or on the item and preceded by a space, diagonal slash, space (see rules 1A1 and 1F1), e.g.:

Best of ol' blue eyes / Frank Sinatra

An economic and social history of Britain since 1700 / by
Michael W. Flynn

Suspended structures / British Constructional Steelwork
Association

Roman Britain / research and text by Colin Barham

The Oxford book of English verse / chosen and edited by Sir Arthur
Quiller-Couch

Typing : first course / Archie Drummond, Anne Coles-Mogford,
with Ida Scattergood

(see reproduction of the chief source of information for this item on
page 5)

The only exception to the above rule is when the name of the responsible person or body has already appeared as part of the title, eg:

The poems of William Wordsworth

Other statements of responsibility that appear in the chief source of information are also given in the form and order in which they appear there. Statements subsequent to the first are introduced by a space, semicolon, space (see rule 1A1), e.g.:

Flowering house plants month by month / by Jack
Kramer ; drawings by Andrew R. Addkison

La vie parisienne : operetta in three acts / Jacques
Offenbach ; music adapted and arranged by Ronald
Hanmer ; new book and lyrics by Phil Park

Usually, qualifications (e.g. academic degrees) and titles of honour or address are omitted from statements of responsibility unless omitting them makes the statement unintelligible or misleading (see rule 1F7).

When a statement of responsibility relates to more than three persons or bodies, all but the first of these are omitted (see rule 1F5). The omission must be indicated by '...' and 'et al.' must be added in square brackets, e.g.:

America's radical right / Raymond Wolfinger ... [et al.]

A word or phrase may be added to the statement of responsibility if it is necessary to make the statement clear, e.g.:

As time goes by / Herman Hupfield ; [sung by] Dooley Wilson

If no statement of responsibility appears in the chief source of information then one is not supplied. If such a statement is necessary to make the description complete then it is given in a note (rule 1F4).

Study rule 1 and then transcribe the titles and statements of responsibility for the following items:

a)

THE HOME MEDICAL ENCYCLOPEDIA

by

David Forsyth, M.R.C.P.

b)

FLIGHT OF FANCY
A History of Aviation

by

J.W. Small P. Winter S. Goody T. Wilson

Turn to frame 34 for the answers.

FRAME 16

The edition statement is transcribed as found in the item but standard abbreviations are used and words are replaced by numbers (see rule 2B), eg:

> 4th ed.   (*not* Fourth edition)
> (see reproduction of the title page on page 5)
> Rev. ed.   (*not* Revised edition)
> U.K. ed.   (*not* United Kingdom edition)

The statement is enclosed in square brackets when it is not taken from a formal statement made by the publisher on the item or in material that accompanies the item (e.g. a record sleeve) (see rule 2A2).

> [New ed.]

When a statement of responsibility relates only to particular editions and not to *all* editions of an item, then it must be included in this area (rule 2C1), e.g.:

> Explaining the atom / by Selig Hecht. — Rev. and with additional chapters / by Eugene Rabinowitch

Examine rule 2C.

On the title page of a book appears:

ANTONY AND CLEOPATRA

William Shakespeare

Edited by

A.E. Morgan, M.A., D.Litt.
and
W. Sherard Vines, M.A.

There is no edition statement in the work. Where would the statement of responsibility relating to the editors be given in the description?

Turn to frame 27 for the answer.

FRAME 17

The special area for serials, computer files, maps and other cartographic materials and music is used to allow for the insertion of information which is specific to each of these materials.

Its use for serials has already been explained (frame 9).

For computer files, it is used as a file characteristic area, e.g.:

	Computer data
or	Computer program

For maps, it is used to present the scale or projection if either of these is found on the item, e.g.:

	Scale 1:63,360
or	Mercator projection

For music, it is used for a musical presentation statement, e.g.:

Playing score

Examine rule 3 and then give the numerical and chronological designations that would appear in this special area for a serial which began publication with volume one in 1978 and ceased publication with volume fifteen in 1992.

Turn to frame 25 for the answer.

FRAME 18

The 'publication, etc.' area has already been partially explained in previous frames. The basic elements consist of the place of publication, publisher and date, e.g.:

New York : Harper, 1991

Generally, only the first named place of publication and first named publisher are included but subsequent places or publishers may be cited in certain instances, for example, if they are given greater prominence in the chief source of information or if they are located in the home country of the cataloguing agency (see rule 4B2).

For example, in a UK library catalogue, the following publication statement might appear:

London : McGraw-Hill

but, in a library catalogue in Australia, this could become:

London ; Sydney : McGraw-Hill
(see the reproduction of the title page on page 5)

The publisher is given in the briefest form in which it can be understood and identified (see rule 4D1), e.g.:

Norman Price (Publishers) Ltd

would be given as:

N. Price

See also the McGraw-Hill example given above.

If the name of the publisher or distributor etc. appears in a recognizable form in a preceding area, it is given in the publication, etc. area in a shortened form (see rule 4D2). The wall chart example in frame 9 illustrates this rule.

In some cases, the name of the publisher, etc may be unknown or even irrelevant. If this is so then this element is omitted.

The date to be given is the date of the edition (see rule 4E1); thus an attempt is made to convey to the catalogue user the currency of the information in an item. The date given is the year in Arabic numbers, e.g.:

1993

The dates of later issues of the same edition are ignored. If information relating to a later issue is considered important (e.g. a reprint of an edition with additions and amendments) then this information could be included in a note (see rule 7B7).

If no date of publication is found on the item then one of the following dates is given (see rule 4E2), in this order of preference:

a) the year of publication found on material accompanying the item, e.g. on a record sleeve;

b) the latest copyright date found on the item, preceded by 'c' or, on some sound recordings, 'p';

c) an approximate date preceded by 'ca.' and enclosed in square brackets.

No matter how approximate, a date must *always* be given. Even [ca.198-], which means 'probably in the 1980s', is better than no date at all.

Examine rule 4E. An item was first published in 1970. A second edition was published in 1978 and a third edition in 1990. The latter was reprinted in 1993. What date would appear in the publication, etc. area of the catalogue description for this reprint?

Turn to frame 37 for the answer.

FRAME 19

The four major elements of the physical description area, as indicated in frame 29, are:

> Extent of item
> Other physical details
> Dimensions
> Accompanying material

The first three elements are obviously the most important. With regard to punctuation, 'Other physical details' are preceded by a space, colon, space, and 'Dimensions' by a space, semi-colon, space (see rule 5A1). Accompanying material(s) is preceded by a space, plus sign, space. Here are a few examples of physical descriptions of various media:

Extent	: Other physical details	; Dimensions
531 p.	: ill. (some col.)	; 25 cm.
1 map	: col.	; 26 x 52 cm.
1 score	: ill.	; 24 cm.
1 sound disc	: digital, stereo.	; 4 3/4 in.
1 sound disc (35 min.)	: analogue, 45 rpm., mono.	; 7 in.
1 film reel (20 min.)	: sd., col.	; 16 mm.
1 art original	: col.	; 45 x 60 cm.
1 computer disk	: col., sd.	; 3 1/2 in.
1 vase	: porcelain, white	; 30 cm. high
v.	: ill.	; 25 cm.
1 microfiche	: ill.	

(Dimensions of microfiche omitted if standard - see rule 5D5)

Note that it is not necessary to specify the type of material that you are cataloguing, i.e. to provide a 'specific material designation', in every case. For instance, the first example above relates to a printed book but this is taken to be implicit by the fact that the number of pages is given. The specific designation for a printed serial is 'v.', preceded by a number if the serial is complete or by three spaces if it is a 'live', incomplete serial.

In the case of nonbook items, the last paragraph of rule 5B1 directs that if the playing time of an item is stated on the item or can be easily ascertained, then the playing time is to be added in parentheses after the specific material designation.

Note also that these examples are merely illustrative of the many possible variations and rule 5 must be consulted for fuller details.

Accompanying material *may* be recorded in the physical description area and, if so, it is preceded by a plus sign, e.g.:

> + 12 slides
> + 1 sound disc

Where accompanying material is minor, it can be described in a note or ignored.

You are required to catalogue a videocassette (VHS with sound and colour) which lasts for 45 minutes. The cassette is 11 x 19 x 3 centimetres in size and it is accompanied by a set of teacher's notes. Refer to rule 5 and formulate a physical description for this item.

Turn to frame 28 for the answer.

FRAME 20

The series area, like other areas, is preceded by a full stop, space, dash, space but, unlike other areas, the series statement is enclosed in parentheses, e.g.:

> (Marketing management series)

Statements of responsibility relating to the series which appear on the item or its container are given if they are necessary for the identification of the series (rule 6C), e.g.:

> (Technical memorandum / Beach Erosion Board)

The number of an item within a series is recorded in the terms given on the item or its container, e.g.:

> (The library series ; 1)
> (Cahiers d'histoire ; no. 20)

Read through rule 6. What information would be included in the series area for an item in which it states that it is both No. 434 of the World Health Organisation's *Technical report series* and No. 81 of the Food and Agricultural Organisation's *Agricultural studies*?

Turn to frame 33 for the answer.

FRAME 21

Notes are intended to amplify or clarify the more formal elements of the description. They may take many forms. Examples of notes are:

> Bibliography: p. 203-215
> Previous ed.: New York : Harper, 1989
> Contents: The man of mode / Sir George Etherege — The country wife / William Wycherley — Love for love / William Congreve
> Available also for Apple Mackintosh
> For 7-9 year olds
> Based on the life of Florence Nightingale

Summary: Shows how the ship was raised after she rolled over and
sank owing to the effects of a fire on board

In general, notes should be as brief as possible (see rule 7A4) and should not repeat information already given in an entry.

Notes are particularly important where media which cannot be 'browsed' (e.g. films) are concerned and they should be freely used. A summary of the content and subject of an item may often be useful.

Notes are presented in an order as laid down in rule 7B. This is basically the order of the areas of the description, i.e. notes on the title, notes on the statement of responsibility, notes on the edition, etc., but preceded by general notes on the nature, scope, form and language of an item.

You are cataloguing a reproduction of a painting, the original of which is in oils and known to be in London's National Portrait Gallery. Is it necessary to include this information in the description and, if so, which form of note from the two listed below would you choose?

> This is a reproduction of the original in oils which is located in the National Portrait Gallery
> Original: oil. In National Portrait Gallery, London

Turn to frame 39 for the answer.

FRAME 22

In the standard number area (see rule 8), the ISBN (International Standard Book Number), ISSN (International Standard Serial Number), or any other internationally agreed number of an item is to be given, e.g.:

> ISBN 0-552-67587-3
> ISSN 0002-9769

Keen-eyed students may have noted that in rule 0D this area is referred to as 'Standard number and terms of availability', but rule 8 does not include any instructions for the latter. Optionally, terms of availability, including the price, could be given if desired. Here are some examples:

> £25.50
> For hire
> Free to members
> Available to the medical profession only

Proceed to next frame.

FRAME 23

Rules 9, 10 and 11 deal, respectively, with 'Supplementary items', 'Items made up of more than one type of material' and 'Facsimiles, photocopies, and other reproductions'.

If a supplementary item has its own title and can be used independently, a separate description is made. Alternatively, the supplementary item is recorded as accompanying material either in the physical description area or in a note.

Items made up of more than one type of material were considered in frame 28.

In describing a facsimile, photocopy, or other reproduction in eye-readable or microform, it is the *facsimile, etc.* that is described and *not* the original. Data relating to the original is given in a note.

Examine rules 9–11 and note the illustrative examples.

This completes our brief study of Part 1 of the *Concise AACR2*, although one further point needs to be made. This is that there will be varying levels of detail in the description according to the requirements of individual libraries and cataloguing agencies. In general, the rules constitute a maximum set of information. For those agencies not requiring this amount of detail, rule 0E of the *Concise AACR2* prescribes a basic, *minimum* level, i.e.:

> Title proper / first statement of responsibility. — Edition statement. — Special area for serials, computer files, maps. — First named publisher, etc., date. — Extent of item. — Required note(s). — Standard number

Even a statement of responsibility can be omitted from the above if the person or body named is the same as that chosen for the main entry heading (see footnote 2 on page 13 of the *Concise AACR2*).

Phase two follows frame 41.

FRAME 24

The areas present in the description of the game are:

> Title area. — Publication area. — Physical description. — Notes

There are no edition, series and standard number areas in this instance.

Proceed to frame 10.

FRAME 25
The answer is (see rule 3A5):

> Vol. 1 (1978)-vol. 15 (1992)

Proceed to frame 18.

FRAME 26
Rule 2A2 instructs that you should take information for this area from the chief source of information or from any formal statement made by the publisher or issuer of the item either on the item or in material which accompanies the item (e.g. a record sleeve). Information taken from elsewhere is enclosed in square brackets.

Proceed to frame 8.

FRAME 27
Rule 2C2 instructs that if there is no edition statement the statement of responsibility relating to an edition is given in the title and statement of responsibility area, i.e.:

> Antony and Cleopatra / William Shakespeare ; edited by A.E.
> Morgan and W. Sherard Vines

Note that the qualifications relating to the editors are omitted in accordance with rule 1F7.

Proceed to frame 17.

FRAME 28
The physical description should be:

> 1 videocassette (45 min.) : sd., col. + 1 set of teacher's notes

The rules that were used are 5B1(l), 5C(5) and 5E2. Rule 5D makes no provision for recording dimensions of videocassettes and therefore none are given. If you were incorrect, re-examine these rules.

The fact that this is a VHS videocassette could be mentioned in a note if desired (i.e. VHS), as it could be considered an important physical detail that is not given in the physical description area (see rule 7B9).

Where 'physical description' is concerned, mention must be made of 'multi-media' items, i.e. those that are made up of two or more components of differing material types. If such an item has one predominant component, it is described in terms of that component; the subsidiary components are treated as accompanying materials and recorded in the physical description area, as indicated in the example above and in frame 19, or given in a note (see the description of the game in frame 9).

However, it may well be that a multi-media item has no predominant component. In this case, the extent of each part, or group of parts, in each class of material must be recorded, followed, if necessary, by a separate physical description for each part or group of parts, e.g. for a tape–slide presentation:

> 25 slides : col.
> 1 sound cassette (15 min.) : analog, mono.

or, for a computer instructional book with linked software:

> 164 p. : ill. ; 22 cm.
> 1 computer disk : col. ; 3 1/2 in.

If an item consists of a large number of different materials, a general term is given, with the number of pieces if it can be easily ascertained, e.g.:

> various pieces
>
> *or*   28 pieces

Items made up of several types of material are dealt with in rule 10.

Examine this rule, and then proceed to frame 20.

FRAME 29

Frame 2 pointed to rule 5 as the relevant rule for the physical description area and this rule indicates that the major elements of the physical description area are:

Extent of item (record the number of parts of an item and the name of the item or parts taken from the list provided in rule 5B), e.g.:

> 1 poster

Other physical details (see rule 5C), e.g.:

> col.

Dimensions (see rule 5D), e.g.:

> 52 x 42 cm.

Accompanying material (see rule 5E), e.g.:

> + 1 booklet

Proceed to frame 5.

FRAME 30

The chief sources of information are:

a) for a map – the item itself;
b) for a computer file – the title screen;
c) here the answer depends upon the medium in which the serial is published. For a printed serial, the chief source is the title page (normally that of the first issue); for a serial issued in the form of a cassette tape, the chief source is the item itself and its labels, and so on.

Examine rule 0A and, where serials are concerned, rule 0B2, before proceeding to frame 7.

FRAME 31

To achieve standardization, each description must consist of the *same basic components*. These components must be cited in the *same order* and be preceded by a *consistent punctuation*.

Proceed to frame 4.

FRAME 32

The answer that you should have is:

>   London : Hamlyn, 1974

or

>   London ; Toronto : Hamlyn, 1974

The first named place is always given as in the first example above. *Optionally*, any other place that is in the country of the cataloguing agency may also be given, as in the second example. The particular cataloguing agency or library must decide on a consistent policy.

If you are incorrect, return to rule 4C2 and re-examine it, noting the way in which the examples have been formulated.

Then proceed to frame 11.

FRAME 33

Rule 6F is the relevant rule, which states that if an item belongs to two or more separate series *and* both are named on the item or its container, then the details of each series are given in the order in which they appear on the item, i.e.:

> (Technical report series / World Health Organisation ;
> no. 434) (Agricultural studies / Food and Agricultural
> Organisation ; no. 81)

Proceed to frame 21.

FRAME 34

The titles and statements of responsibility should be:

a) The home medical encyclopedia / by David Forsyth

b) Flight of fancy : a history of aviation / by J.W. Small ... [et al.]

Note that the titles are transcribed exactly as to wording, order and spelling but not as to capitalization. Note also that the statements of responsibility are recorded as given in the item but that the author's qualifications, etc. are omitted and that when there are more than three persons in a statement of responsibility all but the first of these are omitted. The omission is indicated by three dots and 'et al.' is added in square brackets.

Proceed to frame 16.

FRAME 35

The answer, provided by rule 4B2, is:

> London : CBS Records ; Epic

The first named publisher is always given but if the name of another publisher is more prominent, then that is given also.This sort of problem is commonly encountered where sound recordings are concerned. The label often bears the name of both the publishing company and the name of a subdivision or trade name or brand name used by that company. The full *AACR2* is more helpful in such an instance as it directs that the subdivision or trade name or brand name is to be given as the publisher.

Proceed to frame 12.

FRAME 36

The title statement would be:

>   [Banana]

The title is enclosed in square brackets, denoting that it has been supplied from outside the item. A note on the source of the title is not necessary in this instance, but such a note could also be made, if appropriate, e.g.:

>   Title from container

>   Proceed to frame 14.

FRAME 37

The answer is 1990. If you were incorrect, look again at rule 4E1, noting that the date to be given is the date of the edition, in this case the third edition, 1990, and that later issues of the same edition are to be ignored.

>   Proceed to frame 19.

FRAME 38

The title transcription should be:

>   Out of the dinosaurs : the evolution of the National Lending
>   Library for Science and Technology

If you were wrong, read through frame 12 and rules 1A1, 1B1 and 1E1 again. Refer also to Appendix 1b1 of the *Concise AACR2*. Note that only the first letter of the first word and initial letters of proper adjectives and nouns are capitalized. The other title information is preceded by a space, colon, space.

>   Proceed to frame 13.

FRAME 39

This is information which could be of importance to catalogue users and therefore many libraries and cataloguing agencies would probably decide to include a relevant note. The first note, however, is far too lengthy, repeats information which should have already been given in the earlier parts of the description (i.e. reproduction) and yet fails to say in which National Portrait Gallery the painting is located. The brief, but informative note which should have been selected is:

>   Original: oil. In National Portrait Gallery, London

>   Proceed to frame 22.

FRAME 40

The basic punctuation in the publication area (see rule 4A1) is:

        place : publisher, date
e.g.:   London : Methuen, 1993

Note that each mark of prescribed punctuation is preceded by a space and followed by a space, except for a comma, full stop and opening and closing of parentheses or square brackets.

Proceed to frame 6.

FRAME 41

Check your answer against the following version:

> Improving your garden / by Oliver Dawson. — Rev. ed. —
> London : Pan, 1972. — 165 p. : ill. ; 18 cm. — (Small garden
> series). — Previous ed. published as: Making the most of
> your garden. Feltham : Collingridge, 1967. — ISBN
> 0-330-02896-0

It is likely that most, if not all, of your entry is correct, except perhaps that your note may be differently worded, but this is a relatively minor point at this stage.

Certain abbreviations (ed. for edition, rev. for revised and ill. for illustrated) have been used. Standard abbreviations are permitted by the *Concise AACR2*. Guidance is given at relevant sections of the rules but a full list of permitted abbreviations is not provided (for this, Appendix B of the full *AACR2* must be referred to).

A series statement, as indicated, is enclosed in parentheses; series statements will be dealt with further in a later frame.

Proceed to frame 9.

CHOICE OF ACCESS POINTS

Concise AACR2   Rules 21-29

This is the first section of Part 2 of the *Concise AACR2*. After making a standard description for an item, it is necessary to add access points (name headings and/or titles) to that description, in order to create catalogue entries. This phase and the next one deal with choice of access points and phase four deals with the form that such access points, or headings, may take. The rules considered here apply to all types of library material.

Read the introduction to Part 2, on page 51 of the *Concise AACR2*, before proceeding with this phase.

FRAME 42

Having described an item, *headings* are normally added in order to create catalogue entries. *Headings* provide *access points* in the catalogue. A heading may be a word, name or phrase. It appears at the beginning of the entry and fixes the place of the entry in the catalogue as well as permits the grouping of related entries together.

One possible access point is the title proper of an item and, in this instance, it becomes unnecessary to add a heading, entry being made under the first words of the description.

There is one other addition which may need to be made to a description - a *uniform title*. Uniform titles will be defined, and their use described, in phase five.

The following description was used as an example in frame 8:

> Modern mathematics at Ordinary Level / by L. Harwood
> Clarke. — 2nd ed. — London : Heinemann Educational, 1970. —
> 212 p. : ill. ; 23 cm. — (Heinemann's modern mathematics
> series). — With answers. — ISBN 0-435-50253-0

Possible headings which could be added to this description to provide access points are:

> The person responsible for the work: the heading for L. Harwood
> Clarke
> The series: Heinemann's modern mathematics series

A title entry would also be required: Modern mathematics at Ordinary Level

What, then, might be selected as the headings or access points for the following item?

> Your health / Kenneth C. Hutchin ; illustrated by John
> Barber. — London : Longmans, 1962. — 94 p. : ill. ; 22 cm. —
> (Modern living)

Turn to frame 72 for the answer.

FRAME 43

An important point to note is that rules 21-29 instruct only on methods of selecting access points and *not* on the form that the actual access points, or headings, should take (see rule 21C).

For example, these rules might indicate that one of the access points, or headings, to be used for the book *Strategy* must be the heading for the work's personal author, Sir Basil Liddell Hart, but they will not explain how the name is to be entered. Such an explanation is contained in later rules which will be considered in phase four.

Note, also, that when selecting access points, the chief source of information is to be preferred to other sources. However, it may be necessary to take into account relevant information found elsewhere in or on an item and, when necessary, in reference sources.

Read through rules 21B and 21C and then proceed to next frame.

FRAME 44

The rules for determining the choice of access points in this section also give instructions for the choice of one of these access points as the *main entry* heading. A main entry is that entry where the fullest information is found, presented in a form by which an item can be identified and cited. Other entries then become *added* entries and the headings related to those entries are referred to as added entry headings.

This text assumes that the above principle of main and added entries is to be followed. However, the reader should note that if a particular library or cataloguing agency does not distinguish between main and added entries, all access points selected using rules 21-29 are treated as equal.

Proceed to next frame.

FRAME 45

The main entry heading consists of the name of a *person*, the name of a *corporate body*, or a *title*. The basic rule for determining which of these is to be selected is the general rule 23.

In the case of the names of *persons*, the *Concise AACR2* is primarily concerned with the responsibility for the intellectual or artistic content of an item. For instance, we could be dealing with writers of books; composers of music; artists (sculptors, painters); photographers; compilers of bibliographies; cartographers; and sometimes performers. Is there only one person responsible? Or is responsibility shared? In which case, is there one person principally responsible? etc. The *Concise AACR2* is, therefore, concerned with *conditions* of responsibility or authorship.

Rule 23A2 instructs that a work by one person is entered under the heading for that person. A work by two or more persons is entered under the principal personal author *or* the person named first *or* its title. Various additional rules are provided to help in making a decision as to which to choose.

The *Concise AACR2* defines a *corporate body* as an organization or group of persons that has a name, such as business firms, governments and their agencies, churches, institutions, conferences, and performing groups (rule 23B1). Entry under such bodies is restricted to works which fall into one of the following categories:

a) an administrative work dealing with the corporate body itself (e.g. an annual report), *or* with the body's policies, procedures, etc., *or* its finances, *or* its personnel, *or* its resources;
b) a law or collection of laws, an administrative regulation, a treaty;
c) a report of a committee, commission, etc (providing that the report states the opinion of the committee, etc., and does not merely describe a situation objectively);
d) a liturgical text for which a particular church, denomination, etc., is responsible;
e) a collection of papers given at a conference or the report of an expedition (provided that the conference or expedition is named prominently in the item being catalogued);
f) a sound recording, videorecording, or film created *and* performed by a group;
g) a map or other cartographic material created as well as published by a corporate body.

A work is entered under its *title* (rule 23C) when:

1) the author is unknown *and* no corporate body is responsible;
2) the work has more than three authors *and* none of them is the principal author *and* no corporate body is responsible;
3) it is a collection *or* a work produced under editorial direction *and* has a collective title;
4) it is not by a person or persons *and* is issued by a corporate body *but* is not one of the types of publication listed above;
5) it is a sacred scripture (such as the Bible, the Koran, or the Talmud) *or* an ancient anonymous work (such as *Beowulf* or the *Arabian nights)*.

Examine rule 23 and decide what the main entry heading for each of the following items would be:

a)

POPULAR PET KEEPING

by

P.M. Soderberg

b)

BRITISH MUSEUM

CATALOGUE OF PERSIAN MANUSCRIPTS

c)

Ordnance Survey

ANGLESEY

One-Inch Map

d)   LIBRARY ASSISTANT

The Journal of the
Library Assistants' Association

e)   BUYING A HOUSE?

The Consumer Council
has some advice for you

Turn to frame 81 for the answers.

FRAME 46

Rule 22 gives instructions for dealing with changes of title. A definition of what can be regarded as a change of title is provided in rule 22A and, basically, monographs and serials which may be considered to have changed their titles, in accordance with this definition, have separate main entries made for each change.

Examine this rule. Do you consider that the example included in frame 8, *Improving your garden*, which was previously published as *Making the most of your garden,* constitutes a change of title proper according to the definition included in the rule?

Turn to frame 69 for the answer.

FRAME 47

As was noted in frame 45, the *Concise AACR2* is concerned with *conditions* of responsibility or authorship. The relevant rules for dealing with particular conditions can be ascertained by examining the *Contents* of this section on pages 52 and 53. For instance, it can be seen that rule 24 deals with works for which one person or corporate body is responsible; rule 25 deals with works for which two or more persons or corporate bodies are responsible; rule 26 deals with collections and works produced under editorial direction; and so on. For further guidance, the index to the *Concise AACR2* should be consulted. To use this index, you must not look under, for example, literary forms but under kinds of responsibility (e.g. personal authors).

With this in mind, what would you look up in the index to the *Concise AACR2* to find the appropriate rules for determining responsibility for the following items?

a)   ENCYCLOPAEDIA OF WORLD COOKERY

Elizabeth Campbell

b)   FERODO LIMITED

Friction materials for engineers

Turn to frame 74 for the answer.

FRAME 48

Works for which one person or corporate body is responsible are dealt with in rule 24. A work, collection of works or selections from works by one person is to be entered under the heading for that person, even if he or she is not named in the item being catalogued. A work, collection of works, or selections from a work or works originating from one corporate body is to be entered under the heading for the body *if* the work or collection falls into one or more of the categories given in rule 23B2 (see frame 45).

Study the examples *Encyclopaedia of world cookery* and *Friction materials for engineers* included in the previous frame. According to rule 24 would entry be made under the person and corporate body responsible respectively for each item?

Turn to frame 76 for the answer.

FRAME 49

In solving the problems in frame 48, the reader will have noticed that rule 24B also gives instructions for making added entries in certain instances.

Remember that this section of the *Concise AACR2* is concerned with choice of access points. It follows, therefore, that specific rules will include directions for making added as well as main entry headings. However, the prime concern in this phase is with choice of main entry headings and the remainder of the phase will confine itself to this consideration. We will return, in the next phase, to a study of added entries.

Proceed to next frame.

If directed to read this frame again, proceed to phase three, following frame 86.

FRAME 50

There are bound to be occasions when the person or body responsible for a work remains unknown or uncertain. In such instances rule 23C instructs that the work is entered under its title.

Refer again to rule 23B. If a work originates from a group which lacks a name (e.g., an unnamed conference), then this is also treated as a work of unknown authorship and entered under its title.

Choose main entry headings for the following items:

a) An anonymous work entitled:

THE CHRISTMAS ANTHOLOGY

b) The proceedings of a conference entitled:

JOHN DALTON AND THE PROGRESS OF SCIENCE
Papers presented to a conference of historians of science

Turn to frame 71 for the answers.

FRAME 51
Note that an indication of responsibility does not necessarily have to appear in the item being catalogued. A work by one person is entered under the heading for that person even if he or she is not named in the item (see rule 24A).

The work:

LA VIE DE SAINT AUBAN

an Anglo-Norman poem of the thirteenth century

Edited by Arthur Robert Harden

does not contain any indication of the original author of the poem. Upon checking reference sources, you discover that authorship has been attributed to Matthew Paris. Select a main entry heading for this item.

Turn to frame 73 for the answer.

FRAME 52
There may well be more than one person or body responsible for a work. They could have a similar relationship to the item, for example, they could have written or created it together. This is *shared* authorship or responsibility. When a different relationship exists, for example the work of one person adapted by another person, then this is responsibility of *mixed* character, i.e. an original author and an adapter.

What condition of responsibility is represented by the following item?

THREE PROBLEMS IN FACTORY PLANNING

by

R.F. Baldwin and G.W. Everett

Turn to frame 83 for the answer.

FRAME 53

Shared responsibility is dealt with in rule 25 of the *Concise AACR2*.

Basically, if a *principal* responsibility is indicated, either by wording or layout, then entry is made under the heading for this *principal* person or body. Otherwise, if there are two or three responsible persons or bodies, main entry is made under the one named first. If there are more than three persons or bodies responsible, main entry is under title.

It may well be that principal responsibility is attributed to two or three persons or bodies. In this case, main entry is made under the heading for the first named of these.

Examine rule 25. Under what heading would the main entry for the example cited in the previous frame, *Three problems in factory planning*, appear?

Turn to frame 67 for the answer.

FRAME 54

Again referring to rule 25, choose a main entry heading for the following work:

THE STORY OF THE WORLD'S WORSHIP

by

FRANK S. DOBBINS

assisted by
S. Wells Williams and Isaac Hall

Turn to frame 80 for the answer.

FRAME 55

On the basis of what you have learned so far, choose a main entry heading for the following book:

THE MAKING OF THE WEST INDIES

by

F.R. Augier   S.C. Gordon
D.G. Hall   M. Reckord

Turn to frame 77 for the answer.

FRAME 56

Many works of multiple authorship are produced under the direction of an editor. The *Concise AACR2* directs (rule 26) that such works should be entered under title. Title entry is also to be chosen, according to this rule, for collections of independent works by different persons or bodies, or collections of extracts from such works. In either case, if there is no *collective* title, then entry is made under the heading appropriate to the first work or contribution (rule 26C).

Study rule 26 and choose a main entry heading for each of the following items:

a)
GREAT BRITAIN
GEOGRAPHICAL ESSAYS

Edited by
Jean Mitchell

Each chapter is written by an expert in a particular field.

b)
STUDIES IN COST ANALYSIS

Edited by
David Solomons

The editor states in his preface: 'I have tried to bring together some of the best work done in the field of industrial accounting during the last twenty years'.

c)
AN ANTHOLOGY OF MODERN ANIMAL WRITING

Edited by Frances Pitt

This item consists of samples from the work of twenty to thirty writers.

d)
PILGRIM'S PROGRESS

THE DREAM OF GERONTIUS

PRACTICE OF THE PRESENCE OF GOD

This collection of works, by John Bunyan, Cardinal Newman and Brother Lawrence respectively, although they are not named on the title page, is part of the Bagster's *Christian classics series*.

Turn to frame 86 for the answers.

FRAME 57

We have now considered basic rules for entry of:

1)	Works for which one person or corporate body is responsible	Rule 24;
2)	Works for which two or more persons or corporate bodies are responsible	Rule 25;
3)	Collections and works produced under editorial direction	Rule 26;

The next few frames are designed to test and reinforce your knowledge of these rules. Remember that it may also be necessary to refer to rule 23.

Firstly, decide which of the above conditions relate to each of the following works :

a)

The North Atlantic Treaty Organization

Facts and Figures

b)

THE TRUMPET MAJOR
by
Thomas Hardy
Edited by
Mrs F.S. Boas

c)

CONVERSATIONS BETWEEN

THE CHURCH OF ENGLAND

AND

THE METHODIST CHURCH

d)

THE OXFORD BOOK OF ENGLISH VERSE, 1250-1918

Chosen and Edited by

Sir Arthur Quiller-Couch

e)

RELAX

How You Can Feel Better, Reduce
Stress, and Overcome Tension

EDITED BY JOHN WHITE
AND JAMES FADIMAN

The blurb on the back cover of this work states that: 'a wide range of experts share their secrets for easing tension'.

Turn to frame 79 for the answers.

FRAME 58

Determine the main entry heading for each of the following items:

a)   ZINC ABSTRACTS

This is a monthly publication prepared by the Zinc Development Association / Lead Development Association Abstracting Service;

b)   CHOPIN'S GREATEST HITS

In this album of sound recordings, a noted French pianist and two internationally famous conductors interpret the music of one the great masters;

c)   THE FIGHTING TEMERAIRE

A painting by J.M.W. Turner.

Turn to frame 82 for the answers.

FRAME 59

We have seen that, when considering the conditions of responsibility relating to a particular work, one of the first questions to be asked is whether single authorship or responsibility, shared authorship or responsibility, or mixed responsibility is involved.

A work of mixed responsibility, which has already been mentioned in frame 52, is one that involves the collaboration of two or more persons or bodies *and* to which the persons and/or bodies make different kinds of contribution or perform different kinds of activity, for example, the person or body responsible for the original and a reviser; or, the person or body responsible for the text and an illustrator, and so on.

Such works are dealt with in rule 27. The scope note in rule 27A lists some of the typical instances of mixed responsibility.

For example, the book *Ekorn the squirrel* adapted for children by Ruth Orbach from *Ekorn*, by Haakon Lie, involves authorship of mixed character, viz. an adapter and the original author. One of these must be chosen as the main entry heading. If you consult the index to the *Concise AACR2* under 'Adaptations', you will be referred to rule 27B1(a). If you turn to this rule, you will discover that the work in question is to be entered under the heading for the adaptation, i.e. the heading for the adapter, Orbach.

Which rule would you choose to determine the entry heading for a translation?

Turn to frame 66 for the answer.

FRAME 60

There are two basic categories of mixed responsibility:

i)   where a previously existing work has been modified as with revisions, adaptations or translations;

ii)   a new work produced by persons or bodies making different intellectual or artistic contributions, e.g. a collaborative work between a writer and an artist, or one between a composer and a librettist.

As you may have noticed, the *Concise AACR2* treats these as two separate problems. Rule 27B deals with (i) and rule 27C with (ii).

You are cataloguing the following musical work:

SOUTH PACIFIC

Music by Richard Rodgers

Lyrics by Oscar Hammerstein II

What entries in the index to the *Concise AACR2* would guide you to the relevant rule for selecting the main entry heading for this item?

Turn to frame 85 for the answer.

FRAME 61

The general rule for the entry of a work which is a modification of an existing work is to enter under the heading appropriate to the new work *only* if the nature and content of the original has been changed substantially or if the medium of expression has changed (see the first paragraph of 27B1).

For example, Charles Lamb wrote his *Tales from Shakespeare* in prose rather than verse. This constitutes a change in the medium of expression and entry would be made under the heading for Lamb. Dickens' *Oliver Twist*, retold for boys and girls by Russell Thorndike, contains only a fraction of the original work and the language is very much simplified. Entry is again under the heading appropriate to the new work, i.e. the heading for Thorndike.

Examine rule 27B and then decide on the headings under which entry would be made for the following:

a)   MORSE THEORY

by

J. MILNOR

Based on lecture notes
by M. Spivak and R. Wells

b)   THE STORY OF DAVID COPPERFIELD

BY

CHARLES DICKENS

Abridged by
W. JEWESBURY

The back cover states that this selection of episodes from the original story is told in Dickens' own words.

Turn to frame 75 for the answers.

FRAME 62

Certain media have special problems with regard to 'modification'. Such media include art works, music and sound recordings.

The sorts of problems that are dealt with include:

> adaptations of art works from one medium to another (enter under the adapter - paragraph (d) of 27B1);
>
> arrangements of musical works (enter under the heading for the original work - paragraph (c) of rule 27B2); and
>
> sound recordings of musical or literary works (enter a sound recording of the musical work of one person performed by another under the heading for the original work – paragraph (a) of rule 27B2. However, a sound recording which contains works by different persons or bodies is entered under the principal performer – paragraph (g) of rule 27B1).

Choose main entry headings for the following items:

a) A reproduction of Turner's painting *The fighting Temeraire* made by the firm Athena Reproductions;

b) Music from Beethoven's *Pathétique* arranged by James Last;

c) Frank Sinatra's *Best of ol' blue eyes*, a sound recording of songs by various composers.

Turn to frame 68 for the answers.

FRAME 63

Rule 27C deals with mixed responsibility in new works, for example, a collaboration between artist and writer. Such works are entered under the person or body named first unless the other is given greater prominence by the wording or layout of the chief source of information of the item being catalogued.

Decide what the main entry heading would be under for the following work:

Frederick Wilkinson

GUNS

Illustrated by Michael Shoebridge

Illustrations appear upon almost every page, take up about the same amount of space as the text and are an essential feature of the work.

Turn to frame 70 for the answer.

FRAME 64

A work which has a relationship to some other work, such as a supplement, an index, a concordance, a libretto, a screenplay, or a special number of a serial, etc., is entered under its own heading and *not* the heading for the work to which it is related. This provision is dealt with in the rule for *related* works – rule 28. It should be remembered that for particular types of relationships, such as revisions and translations, rule 27 should be used.

According to rule 28, Cruden's concordance to the Bible would, for instance, be entered under Cruden.

Decide upon main entry headings for:

a)

SPECTATOR'S CHOICE

Articles reprinted from *The Spectator*

Edited by George Hutchinson

b)

WILLIAMS ON THE LAW AND PRACTICE RELATING

TO THE CONTRACT FOR SALE OF LAND AND THE

TITLE TO LAND

2nd (Cumulative) Supplement

by

R.T. Oerton

Turn to frame 78 for the answers.

FRAME 65

To complete this study of choice of access points, choose the appropriate main entry heading for each of the following:

a)   GREENBANK HIGH SCHOOL FOR GIRLS
                    Parents' Handbook

b)   FACE TO FACE

                        A Film

                          by

                   INGMAR BERGMAN

           Translated from the Swedish by Alan Blair

This is a film which was subsequently published in book form.

c)   British Library Act 1972

d)   THE SPINNERS

                    The Singing City

A sound recording of the group The Spinners singing songs relating to Liverpool and the North West of England.

e)   James Joyce's Ulysses

                       A Study

                   by Stuart Gilbert

Described in the preface as a commentary and only selected passages from *Ulysses* are included.

f)   Radio Times

                   STEP-BY-STEP

                    ALL-COLOUR

                     COOKBOOK

                     John Tovey

The best of the recipes from John Tovey's weekly cookery column in the *Radio times*.

g) ## BIRDS OF THE ATLANTIC OCEAN
Paintings by Keith Shackleton

Text by Ted Stokes

Foreword by H.R.H. The Prince Philip,
Duke of Edinburgh

h) Lawrence Nathan's

CAR DRIVING IN TWO WEEKS

Revised, added to, modernised and re-written by

ANDREW M. HUNT

Turn to frame 84 for the answers.

FRAME 66

The relevant rule, found by consulting the index to the *Concise AACR2* under 'Translations', is 27B2(b).

Proceed to frame 60.

FRAME 67

The answer is the heading for R.F. Baldwin. When there are not more than three persons or bodies responsible and a principal responsibility is not indicated, entry is under the first named (see rule 25C1).

Proceed to frame 54.

FRAME 68

The appropriate main entry headings are those for:

a) Turner

There has been no substantial change to the original art work – see the introductory paragraph of rule 27B1;

b) Beethoven

Rule 27B2(c) applies;

c) Sinatra

Rule 27B1(g) applies.

Return to the rules indicated, if you were incorrect, to see how these answers have been obtained, then proceed to frame 63.

FRAME 69

Words have been deleted and added (rule 22A, first paragraph) and this does, therefore, constitute a change of title proper according to the definition.

Proceed to frame 47.

FRAME 70

Where a work is the result of collaboration between an artist and a writer, entry is under the heading for the one named first unless the other's name is given greater prominence. In this instance entry is, therefore, under the heading for Wilkinson, the author of the text.

Proceed to frame 64.

FRAME 71

A work of unknown authorship, such as *The Christmas anthology*, is entered under title. *John Dalton and the progress of science* is also entered under title, as this is a work by an unnamed group.

The above decisions were taken in accordance with rule 23C, but 23B2 is also relevant in the latter case. The corporate body concerned, which is also a conference, is considered not to have a name because initial letters are not capitalized and the indefinite article is used.

Proceed to frame 51.

FRAME 72

The headings or access points that would be required are:

The person responsible for the work: the heading for Kenneth C. Hutchin
The title: Your health
The series: Modern living

A further possible access point is the heading for the illustrator, John Barber, but, as will be seen later, whether an entry is made or not will depend upon how much prominence is given to the illustrator in the work and upon how extensive and important the illustrations are.

Turn to frame 43.

FRAME 73

Entry would be under the heading for Matthew Paris, even though he is not named in the item (rule 24A).

Proceed to frame 52.

FRAME 74

The *Encyclopaedia of world cookery* is a work by one 'personal author' and this is the *condition* of authorship which should be consulted in the index to the *Concise AACR2*. Note that it is totally wrong to attempt to find a rule for entering the *type* of publication and the term 'encyclopaedias' does not appear in the index to the rules.

Friction materials for engineers is a work originating from a single 'corporate body' and this is the *condition* which should be looked for in the index, i.e. 'Corporate bodies, entry under'.

Proceed to frame 48.

FRAME 75

Rule 27B1 is applicable to (a). The work is a modification of original lecture notes and the wording of the title page appears to indicate that the persons responsible for the original are no longer responsible for the work. Entry would, therefore, be made under the heading for Milnor.

Item (b) is covered by paragraph (e) of rule 27B2, an abridgement being entered under the heading appropriate to the original, i.e. the heading for Dickens.

Proceed to frame 62.

FRAME 76

The *Encyclopaedia of world cookery* would be entered under the single person responsible according to rule 24A. *Friction materials for engineers* is, however, a work originating from a corporate body which does not fall within the categories given in rule 23B2. It does not, therefore, come within the compass of rule 24B but would be entered under title according to rule 23C.

Proceed to frame 49.

FRAME 77

When there are more than three persons or bodies responsible and principal responsibility is not indicated, entry is under title (rule 25C2).

Proceed to frame 56.

FRAME 78

A related work is to be entered under its own heading according to rule 28. *Spectator's choice* must, therefore, be treated as a collection and would be entered under title according to the provisions of rule 26B. Item (b), the supplement, is a work of a single personal author and would be entered under the heading for Oerton according to the provisions of rules 23A and 24A.

Proceed to frame 65.

FRAME 79

The conditions are:

a) Single corporate body responsible (i.e. North Atlantic Treaty Organization). Rule 24B applies. Rule 23B2 is also relevant as this work would be considered to be one of an administrative nature dealing with the body itself;
b) Single person responsible. Rule 24A applies. The fact that there is an editor is irrelevant in this instance. This is the work of one person, i.e. Hardy;
c) Shared responsibility. Category (4) of rule 25A applies. Note that rule 23B2 must also be considered before rule 25C1 can be used;
d) This is a collection of extracts from independent works by different persons produced under editorial direction (rule 26A – category (1));
e) This is a work consisting of contributions by different persons produced under editorial direction (rule 26A – category (2)).

Proceed to frame 58.

FRAME 80

The answer is the heading for Dobbins as he is the *principal* person responsible. This can be indicated by either wording or layout. In this case both are used: the wording says *by* Dobbins *assisted by* Williams and Hall; the layout presents DOBBINS in larger, capitalized type (see rule 25B1).

If you were wrong, go over the example again and make sure that you understand it before proceeding.

The item for which the chief source of information is reproduced on page 5 is another example where the wording of the title page indicates principal responsibility. In this case it is attributed to *two* persons – Drummond and Coles-Mogford. Main entry would be under the heading for the first of these (see frame 53 and rule 25B2).

Proceed to frame 55.

FRAME 81

The main entry headings would be:

a) The heading for P.M. Soderberg;
b) The heading for the British Museum;
c) The heading for the Ordnance Survey;
d) Library assistant;
e) Buying a house?;

In the case of (a), entry is made under the single person responsible for the work (rule 23A2 and 24A). In the case of (b) and (c), entry will be under the single corporate body responsible for each of the works. Item (b) falls within category (a) of rule 23B2, as it is a catalogue describing the resources of the corporate body. (c) is a cartographic item emanating from a corporate body which is responsible for creating as well as publishing the item (see rule 23B2(g)).

The *Library assistant* (d) and *Buying a house?* (e) also emanate from corporate bodies but, in these instances, the items do not fall within any of the categories listed in rule 23B2 and therefore entry is under title according to the provisions of rule 23C.

Proceed to frame 46.

FRAME 82

The main entry headings would be:

a) The title: Zinc abstracts;
b) The heading for Chopin;
c) The heading for Turner;

(a) originates from a corporate body but does not fall into one of the categories given in rule 23B2. It is therefore entered under title according to rule 23C. Rule 24B is not relevant in this particular instance.

In the case of (b) and (c), a single person is responsible for the intellectual or artistic content. Rules 23A and 24A apply.

This completes the short test of your knowledge of the basic rules.

Proceed to frame 59.

FRAME 83

This is *shared* responsibility, which occurs when more than one person or body have a similar relationship to the work.

Proceed to frame 53.

FRAME 84

The main entry headings would be:

a) The heading for the school
   This is a work of an administrative nature originating from a corporate body and dealing with the body itself – rules 23B2 and 24B;

b) The heading for Bergman
   This is a translation and is therefore entered under the heading for the original work – rule 27B2(b);

c) The heading for the United Kingdom
   This is a law governing one jurisdiction and is entered under the heading for the jurisdiction governed – rule 24B;

d) The heading for The Spinners
   This is a sound recording performed by a group – rule 23B2(f). Rule 27B1(g) is also relevant – a sound recording of works by different persons performed by a principal performer;

e) The heading for Gilbert
   A commentary is entered under the heading for the new work – rule 27B1(c)

f) The heading for Tovey
   This is a related work which is entered under its own heading – rule 28B (see the *Saturday review of literature* example). An added entry would be made under *Radio times*;

g) The heading for Shackleton
   This is a work of mixed responsibility resulting from the collaboration between an artist and a writer. Such a work is entered under the one named first unless the other is given greater prominence – rule 27C;

h) The heading for Hunt
   The original author is named only in the title proper and the original work has apparently been considerably modified and adapted – rule 27B1(b).

This completes our introductory study of 'Choice of access points' except for 'Added entries'. These will be dealt with in the next phase but, before proceeding, return to frame 49 and re-read it.

FRAME 85

The musical *South Pacific* is a work of collaboration between the composer of the music and the lyricist, or librettist. The relevant index entries are:

> Composers
> > collaborations with librettists

and

> Librettists, collaborations with
> > composers

Both of these entries point to rule 27C.

Proceed to frame 61.

FRAME 86

Item (a) is a work of multiple authorship produced under the direction of an editor. Items (b) and (c) consist of independent works, or extracts from such works, which have been collected together by an editor. In all three of these instances, rule 26 directs that main entry should be under title. Item (d), however, does not have a collective title and is, therefore, entered under the heading appropriate to the first work. This would be the heading for the single person responsible, i.e. that for John Bunyan.

Proceed to frame 57.

CHOICE OF ACCESS POINTS

ADDED ENTRIES

Mentioned throughout rules 21 to 28 of the *Concise AACR2* and specifically covered in rule 29

FRAME 87

A user may make many approaches when searching for a particular item: the 'author' approach, the 'title' approach, the 'series' approach, etc. All of these various types of entry headings, or access points, must be considered by the indexer.

In the last phase, we were concerned primarily with the choice of main entry headings, although, as was noted in frame 49, rules 21 to 28 also indicate the added entries that are required in the particular circumstances with which each rule deals. For example, rule 26B, referring to works produced under editorial direction, tells us to make added entries for the editor or editors (depending upon how many there are). Thus, for the work *Relax*, which was used as an example in frame 57 and which would be entered under its collective title, added entries would be made under both of the editors.

An examination of rule 29 indicates that, in general, an added entry may be made under any heading (for a person, corporate body or title) if that heading might be used by some users of the catalogue rather than the main entry heading. In other words, an entry may be made under any heading that could be important for retrieval purposes.

The following items were used as examples of shared authorship in frames 54 and 55:

a)   THE STORY OF THE WORLD'S WORSHIP

by

FRANK S. DOBBINS
assisted by
S. Wells Williams and Isaac Hall

b)   THE MAKING OF THE WEST INDIES

by

F.R. Augier   S.C. Gordon
D.G. Hall   M. Reckord

As explained in frames 80 and 77, in the case of (a) main entry would be under the principal author Dobbins, and in the case of (b) main entry would be under title. What added entries would be needed?

Turn to frame 94 for the answers.

FRAME 88

When considering conditions of responsibility, as well as single responsibility or shared responsibility, a work may be the result of authorship or responsibility of *mixed* character (see also frame 59). Rule 27 deals with this problem and it may involve modification of an existing work (rule 27B) or the production of a new work by persons or bodies making different intellectual or artistic contributions (27C).

Usually, for modifications of existing works, if main entry is under the heading for the new work, an added entry is made for the original (see rule 27B1). If main entry is under the original work, an added entry is made for the modifier, performer, reviser, etc.

For new works, if there are three or fewer collaborating persons or bodies, then added entries are made for those persons or bodies not selected as the main entry heading. If there are more than three persons or bodies, and none is given prominence, then main entry would be under title and an added entry would be made under the person or body named first (see rule 27C).

In frame 59, we also looked at the rule for translations. A translation is a modification of an existing work and entry would, in this case, be under the heading for the original – rule 27B2(b). Whether an added entry is to be made under the translator depends upon certain factors and in rule 27B2(b) you are directed to rule 29B6 for further elaboration.

Examine these two rules and decide whether an added entry would be necessary for Leonard Tancock as translator of Zola's *Thérèse Raquin* into English. This work has also been translated into English by various other people.

Turn to frame 96 for the answer.

FRAME 89

Find the appropriate rule number for added title entries. Would an added title entry be necessary for each of the following titles?

a) The language of Shakespeare / N.F. Blake
b) The Shakespeare handbook / edited by Levi Fox
c) Shakespeare's complete works
d) Shakespearean tragedy : lectures ... / by A.C. Bradley

Turn to frame 95 for the answers.

FRAME 90

Find the appropriate rule number for series added entries. Would an added entry be necessary for each of the following series?

a) *British Parliamentary papers*
b) *Living Shakespeare* – a series of sound recordings of Shakespeare's plays
c) *Young Puffins* – a series which includes many stories for younger children, such as *Paddington helps out*, by Michael Bond

Turn to frame 99 for the answers.

FRAME 91

Why would the main entry for the following work be under the heading for Barry Williams? Would added entries be necessary for:

    a) the illustrator?
    b) the title?
    c) the series?

CARAVANNING

BARRY WILLIAMS

Illustrated by Tri-Art

The illustrations occupy more than fifty per cent of the item. The book is one of the 'TV times family books' series.

Turn to frame 97 for the answers.

FRAME 92

Return to the Oerton example used in frame 64. Would an added entry be required for the work to which this item is related?

Turn to frame 100 for the answer.

FRAME 93

The example *Modern mathematics at Ordinary Level* was used in frame 8 and possible access points were considered in frame 42. Return to frame 42 and decide which of these access points must be chosen as the main entry heading. Which of the other possible access points would require added entries?

Turn to frame 98 for the answer.

FRAME 94

The relevant rules for shared responsibility are 25B, where principal responsibility is indicated, and 25C where it is not. In the case of (a), added entries would be made under the headings for the other persons, as there are not more than two (see rules 25B1 and 29B1). In the case of (b), an added entry would be made only for the first person named (see rules 25C2 and 29B1).

In the case of (a), an added entry would also be necessary under the title (see rules 29A2 and 29B5).

The required entries would therefore be:

(a) Main entry: the heading for Dobbins
    Added entries: the heading for Williams
                    the heading for Hall
                    title

(b) Main entry: title
    Added entries: the heading for Augier

Proceed to frame 88.

FRAME 95

Rule 29B5 is the appropriate rule number for added title entries. According to this rule, added entry under title would be necessary for (a) *The language of Shakespeare* and (d) *Shakespearean tragedy : lectures* ... In the case of (b), *The Shakespearean handbook*, this is a work produced under editorial direction and, therefore, the *main* entry would be under title (did you spot this?). Main entry for (c) would be under the heading for Shakespeare and, as the title proper is essentially the same as this main entry heading, no added entry would be necessary (see rule 29B5(a)).

Proceed to frame 90.

FRAME 96

An added entry under the translator would be necessary because the work has been translated into the same language more than once (rule 29B6(a)(ii) applies).

Proceed to frame 89.

FRAME 97

The main entry would be under the heading for Barry Williams because he is given greater prominence by the layout of the chief source of information (see rule 27C). It would still be Williams even if he were not given prominence because he is named first. An added entry would be necessary for the illustrator, Tri-Art, because the illustrations occupy more than half the text (see rule 29B6(b)(ii)). Added entries would also be necessary for the title (see rule 29B5) and for the series (see rule 29B7 – the added entry would seem to provide a useful grouping of entries).

Proceed to frame 92.

FRAME 98

The main entry heading would be the heading for Clarke, as he is the single person responsible for the content of the work (rules 23A and 24A). Added entries would be needed under the title (according to rule 29B5) and under the series (according to rule 29B7).

You should now know enough about the *Concise AACR2*'s treatment of added entries to be able to apply the relevant rules. Remember that, when in doubt about the interpretation of a particular rule, it is better to make an added entry rather than not make one. Remember also that the rules provide guidelines only. It is possible, as indicated in frame 87, to make an added entry for *any* access point which you consider may be 'sought'.

One last point, as previously indicated in frame 44, is that some catalogues are based upon the principle of *alternative headings*; the various headings required are simply added above the standard description and no attempt is made to distinguish between main and added entries. For such catalogues, rules 21 to 29 can still be used as a guide to the headings that should be selected as access points (see the General introduction to the *Concise AACR2*).

Proceed to phase four, following frame 100.

FRAME 99

The appropriate rule number for series added entries is 29B7. In the case of (a) and (b), *British Parliamentary papers* and *Living Shakespeare*, a series added entry would seem to provide a useful grouping of entries according to the wording of this rule. In the case of (c), *Young Puffins*, a series added entry would not seem to provide a useful grouping as there are so many titles in this series and the series title merely appears to indicate a Puffin publication for younger readers.

Proceed to frame 91.

FRAME 100

Yes, an added entry would be required for the work to which the Oerton supplement is related (rule 29B4 applies).

Another example of an occasion when an added entry would be required under a related work, can be found in frames 65 and 84 (example (f) – *Step-by-step all-colour cookbook*, recipes from the *Radio times*). An added entry under the *Radio times*, the work to which the item is related, is needed according to rule 29B4.

Proceed to frame 93.

HEADINGS

Concise AACR2   Rules 30–44 Persons
                          Rules 45–47 Geographic names
                          Rules 48–56 Corporate bodies

FRAME 101

Having chosen the access points, or headings, under which a particular item is to be entered in the catalogue, problems may still be encountered with regard to *how* such headings are to be entered. For example, if, using rules 21–29, it is decided that an entry is to be made under Mao Tse-tung, which part of the name will come *first* in the heading? Some guidance is needed.

Headings for *persons* are dealt with in rules 30–44;
Headings for *geographic names* are dealt with in rules 45–47;
Headings for *corporate bodies* are dealt with in rules 48–56.

Proceed to next frame.

FRAME 102

In rules 30–44 (headings for persons), there are basically two problems involved:

i) The first problem relates to the different names or different forms of name by which a person might be known.

For example, Harry Webb performs as a singer under the different name of Cliff Richard, and the name of the playwright Shaw appears in various forms in his works, i.e. Bernard Shaw, George Bernard Shaw and G.B. Shaw.

Advice is needed on which of these different names or different forms of name should be chosen as the basis for the entry heading.

ii) The second problem relates to the way in which the chosen name is to be entered.

Names such as compound names, names with prefixes, foreign names, etc., may be confusing or unfamiliar. The name used in frame 101, Mao Tse-tung, is one example.

Advice may be required as to which part to select as the entry element.

Where problem (i) is concerned, in accordance with the general structure of the *Concise AACR2*, the first basic rule (rule 31A) is prepotent. This states that a person is entered under the name by which he or she is *commonly known*. This is most important and thus we would choose, as a basis for headings, names such as:

Dizzy Gillespie *not* John Birks Gillespie
George Eliot *not* Mary Ann Evans
George Orwell *not* Eric Arthur Blair
John Wayne *not* Marion Michael Morrison

The following names would not be those chosen for these people because they are more commonly known by other names. Do you know what those other names are?

Norma Jean Baker
Samuel Langhorne Clemens
David John Moore Cornwell
Charles Edouard Jeanneret
Tiziano Vecelli

Turn to frame 119 for the answers.

FRAME 103

In the light of what you have learned so far, what would be the heading that you would choose for the author H.G. Wells;

Herbert George Wells
or   H G Wells
or   H.G. Wells

Turn to frame 125 for the answer.

FRAME 104

The rules following the prepotent rule, 31A, cover the two basic problems indicated in frame 102.

The first of these problems is that of a person known by different names or by different forms of name. Rules 31B to 31D and 32 deal with this problem. Rule 31 is the general rule and rule 32 deals more specifically with choice among different names.

Rule 31B states that if a person is identified by a name that contains a surname then the form of name to be used is that which appears in the chief source of information (e.g. the title page of a book) of works by that person in his or her language. This rule will cover the vast majority of the cases which will be encountered. Note that some of the examples used in previous frames, George Eliot, George Orwell and H.G. Wells, are forms of name which contain a surname and which fall into this category. These are the forms of name which appear in these authors' works.

The comedian and author Terence Alan Milligan uses the name Spike Milligan in works such as *Military memoirs* or *Puckoon*. The tennis player R.A. Gonzales wrote his autobiography *Man with a racket* under the name Pancho Gonzales. Teodor Josef Konrad Korzeniowski wrote his novels, such as *Lord Jim*, under the name Joseph Conrad. Which forms of these names would you choose as a basis for entry headings?

Turn to frame 130 for the answers.

FRAME 105

If the chief source of information is of little or no help (as, for example, with a piece of sculpture), or if the person is not primarily known as a creator of works (as, for example, with politicians and film actors), the form of name to be used is that found in reference sources, other books, and articles issued in the person's language or country (rule 31B1(b)).

Imagine that you are cataloguing a reproduction of *The Thinker*, a piece of sculpture. The surname of the sculptor, Rodin, is given on the piece. How would you ascertain the form of name to be used as an entry heading?

Turn to frame 127 for the answer.

FRAME 106

Sometimes you may be required to formulate a heading for a person identified by a name that does not contain a surname. The name to be used is that by which he or she is identified in English-language reference sources which are available to you (rule 31B2(a)), e.g.:

> Alcuin
> Alfred the Great
> Saint Francis
> Pope Pius XII
> Sitting Bull

If the name cannot be found in English-language reference sources, the form of name to be used is that which appears in the chief sources of information of works by the particular person in his or her language (rule 31B2(b)), e.g.:

> A.L.O.E.
> Vatsyayana

Whether the name contains a surname or not, titles of royalty, nobility, or terms of honour that usually appear as part of the name are to be included (rule 31C), e.g.:

> Prince Philip
> Sir Walter Scott
> Count Alexei Nikolaevich Tolstoi

If the name contains a surname, terms other than those noted above are to be omitted (rule 31D, first paragraph), e.g.:

> Joseph O'Leary *not* Father Joseph O'Leary
> Robert Scott *not* Captain Robert Scott

However, if the name does not contain a surname *or* if it consists of only a surname and a word or phrase, terms that normally appear as part of the name are to be included (rule 31D, second paragraph), e.g.:

> Drunken Barnaby
> Dr. Seuss

Read through rule 31 and then consider the cataloguing problems posed by the following items. Decide on your choice of heading in each case:

a) A book on the title page of which appears *Britain's glorious navy* edited by Admiral Sir Reginald H.S. Bacon K.G.B., K.C.V.O., D.S.O.;

b) A work *Nursery rhymes of Gloucestershire*, on the title page of which appears 'by E.R.P.B.' This name cannot be found in the reference sources available to you;

c) The novel *John Halifax, gentleman* on the title page of which appears 'by Mrs. Craik'.

Turn to frame 126 for the answers.

FRAME 107

A common instance of a person using different names is that of an author, performer, etc. who adopts a pseudonym or pseudonyms for all or some of his works or performances. We have already considered some examples, e.g. John Le Carré, Cliff Richard and Mark Twain. The relevant rule is 32A and this rule conforms to the basic, general rule, in that if a person always uses the *one* pseudonym, entry is under that pseudonym.

When two or more collaborators use one pseudonym, entry is under that pseudonym (32A1). For example, Ellery Queen is the joint pseudonym of Frederic Dannay and Manfred B. Lee.

The entertainer Jeanne Bourgeois, known as Mistinguett, is probably the most famous star in the history of the French music hall. Which name, Bourgeois or Mistinguett, would you choose as the basis of a heading for this person when entering her autobiography? The title page says:

MISTINGUETT
QUEEN OF THE PARIS NIGHT

Turn to frame 128 for the answer.

FRAME 108

A person may have established two or more bibliographic identities, as indicated by the fact that works of one type appear under one pseudonym and works of other types appear under other pseudonyms or the person's real name. For example, Charles Lutwidge Dodgson wrote his children's stories as Lewis Carroll; and Cecil Day Lewis wrote detective stories as Nicholas Blake. Each group of works is entered under the name by which it is identified in the chief sources of information of the particular type of work. Where contemporary authors are concerned, if a person uses more than one pseudonym (or a real name and one or more pseudonyms), each item is entered according to the name appearing in it (rule 32A2).

If a person using more than one pseudonym (or a real name and one or more pseudonyms):

> *neither* has established separate bibliographical identities;
> *nor* is a contemporary author,

choose the name by which that person has come to be identified in later editions of his or her works, in critical works, and/or in reference sources (rule 32A2, last paragraph)). For some years, Walter Scott's novels were published as 'by the author of *Waverley*' but, if cataloguing one of these works today, entry would be under Scott. Charles Dickens used the pseudonym Boz in the first edition of *Pickwick papers*, but this work would now be entered under Dickens.

Sir Kingsley Amis writes poetry and novels, but his enthusiasm for Ian Fleming's work expressed itself in *The James Bond dossier* and *Colonel Sun*, which he wrote under the name Robert Markham. What would you choose as the basis of the heading for these latter two works?

Turn to frame 123 for the answer.

FRAME 109

When a person uses more than one pseudonym, or a real name and one or more pseudonyms, and different names for such a person appear in different editions of the same work *or* if two or more names appear in the same edition, choose (in this order of preference) – rule 32A2:

> the name that has appeared most frequently in editions of the work;
> the name appearing in the latest edition of the work.

Proceed to next frame.

FRAME 110

If a person does not use a pseudonym, but is still known by more than one name or more than one form of name, the name to be chosen as the basis for the entry heading is that by which the person is clearly most commonly known. This conforms to the general rule and we have already seen examples of the application of this rule. Cassius Clay would be entered under his now, better-known, name Mohammad Ali; and Terence Alan Milligan would be entered under the better-known form Spike Milligan.

If there is no name by which the person is more commonly known, choose (in this order of preference):

> the name that appears most frequently in issues of the person's works;
> the name that appears most frequently in current reference sources;
> the latest name.

Examine rule 32B, carefully noting the examples (which include the Mohammad Ali example noted above).

In *The Oxford companion to English literature*, the Roman comic poet Publius Terentius Afer is entered as Terence; which of these forms of name would you use if you were cataloguing one of his works?

Turn to frame 121 for the answer.

FRAME 111

So far we have been concerned only with the problem of which name to choose as a basis for an entry heading when a person is identified by different names or different forms of name. Let us now look at the second major problem relating to headings for persons – the selection of the entry element.

The general rule (33) instructs that when a person's name consists of more than one part, one of these parts is to be chosen as the entry element, that is the part under which the heading is to be filed and/or retrieved.

If the entry element is the first part of the name, the name is to be entered in direct order, e.g.:

San Antonio

If the entry element is not the first part of the name, the name is inverted (rule 33A2). Thus:

William Shakespeare

becomes

Shakespeare, William

Note that the entry lead element is followed by a comma.

Proceed to next frame.

FRAME 112

The most obvious example of a name which requires inversion is a name which contains a surname (as in the Shakespeare example in the previous frame). The reader will probably have already reasoned that names would not be entered as in the examples we have previously cited, that is as:

> Spike Milligan
>
> *or*   H.G. Wells

Clearly, if a name contains a surname, entry must be under the surname, e.g.:

> **Milligan, Spike**
>
> *and*   **Wells, H.G.**

Rule 34A is the relevant rule for entry under surname. However, not all surnames consist of a single name and other problems may need to be considered. These problems include:

> Hyphenated names such as Anne Coles-Mogford (this name appears on the title page reproduced on page 5)
>
> Compound surnames, such as Ralph Vaughan Williams
>
> Names with separately written prefixes, such as the name of the Dutch author Michel van der Plas

Carefully examine rule 34 and then decide on the headings that you would choose for the above three authors.

Turn to frame 129 for the answers.

FRAME 113

Note that rule 34C5 caters for instances when the nature of the surname is uncertain. Examine this rule and decide on the form of heading that you would use for Julia Trevelyan Oman.

Turn to frame 120 for the answer.

FRAME 114

The problem of different names or different forms of name is also evident where a title of nobility is concerned. A nobleman may be entered under his title or his family surname. The basic, general rule is the one to remember here, and the key is how the person is commonly identified. Thus the Duke of Wellington would be entered under his better-known *title* and not under his *family name*.

As in the Duke of Wellington example, the acquisition of a title can involve a change of name, but it may well be that the earlier name continues to be the better-known one. For example:

Benjamin Disraeli

not   Earl of Beaconsfield

If there is no better-known name, the instructions in rule 32B (see frame 110) are to be followed.

Titles of nobility are specifically dealt with in rule 35, but are also mentioned in rules 31C and 33A3. Read through these rules.

Proceed to next frame.

FRAME 115

Rules 36, 37, 38 and 39 deal respectively with entry under given name, entry of Roman names, entry under initials, letters or numerals and entry under phrase. We have already met examples of these names, i.e.:

Saint Francis of Assisi

Publius Terentius Afer

E.R.P.B.

and   Drunken Barnaby

Examine these rules and formulate appropriate headings for the above persons.

Turn to frame 124 for the answers.

FRAME 116

Rules 40 to 44 provide for additions to names in certain circumstances.

Rule 40 deals with titles of nobility and British terms of honour.

As previously indicated, a nobleman or noblewoman may be entered under their *title* or under their *family surname*. Where such a person is not entered under title but under the family name, the title of nobility may be added if the title or part of the title commonly appears with the name in works by the person or in reference sources. We have seen an example of this in Count Tolstoy (see frame 106), who would be entered thus:

Tolstoi, Alexei Nikolaevich, *Count*

An example of a nobleman entered under his better-known family name is Patrick Campbell, who was Baron Glenavy. As he was not commonly known by this title, and did not use it in his works, he would be entered simply as:

Campbell, Patrick

Proceed to next frame.

FRAME 117

Rule 41 provides for making additions to names that do not appear to be the names of persons. In such instances, suitable English designations are to be added in parentheses, e.g.:

Taj Mahal *(Musician)*
Sting *(Singer)*
River *(Writer)*

This is not a very common occurrence where a single personal name is concerned.

Proceed to next frame.

FRAME 118

Rules 42 and 43, which also cater for additions to names, are very important in that they provide for distinguishing between names which are otherwise the same. There are two ways in which this can be achieved. If a person is identified by a name that contains or consists of initials, and the fuller form is known, the spelled-out names may be added in parentheses. Dates of birth and/or death may also be added to distinguish between otherwise identical headings.

You are required to distinguish between two authors, both of whom write under the name Alice B. Johnson. Upon checking reference sources, you discover that the B. stands for Barbara in each case. You also find that one author was born in 1961 and is still living; the other died in 1968. What forms of heading would you use?

Turn to frame 122 for the answers.

FRAME 119

Norma Jean Baker is better known as the film star Marilyn Monroe;
Samuel Langhorne Clemens as the author Mark Twain;
David John Moore Cornwell as the author John Le Carré;
Charles Edouard Jeanneret as the architect Le Corbusier;
Tiziano Vecelli as the painter Titian.

Did you know all of these? Probably not, which illustrates the reasoning behind entry being made under the name by which a person is commonly known. Rule 31A directs that entry for each of the above would be under the better-known name.

Proceed to frame 103.

FRAME 120

The correct form of heading is:

Oman, Julia Trevelyan

If a name appears to contain a compound surname, but you are not sure, entry should be under the last part of the name if the person's language is English or one of the Scandinavian languages. Otherwise entry is under the first part.

Proceed to frame 114.

FRAME 121

The answer is the heading for Terence. This is clearly the name by which this person is commonly known (rules 31A and 32B) and also the name by which he is identified in English-language reference sources (see the Horace example in rule 31B2).

Proceed to frame 111.

FRAME 122

The forms of heading are:

Johnson, Alice B. (Alice Barbara), *1961-*
Johnson, Alice B. (Alice Barbara), *d.1968*

If you were wrong re-examine rules 42 and 43, carefully noting the illustrative examples.

Note also that rule 44 stipulates that if neither a fuller form of name nor dates are available, you must not add anything and the headings are interfiled.

Proceed to frame 131.

FRAME 123

The answer is the heading for Robert Markham. This is a contemporary author using a real name and a pseudonym (rule 32A2). Entry is made under the name found in a particular work. This example also conforms to the rule that relates to a person who has published one group of works under one name and another group under another name.

Keen-eyed students may have noted that *Colonel Sun* is also a related work and, in this regard, it is used as an example in rule 28B of the *Concise AACR2*.

Proceed to frame 109.

FRAME 124

The appropriate headings are:

Francis, *of Assisi, Saint*
Where given names are concerned, entry is under the part of the name by which the person is listed in reference sources. Words or phrases usually associated with the name are included in the heading (rule 36).

Terence
A Roman of classical times is entered under that part of the name most commonly used as the entry element in modern reference sources (rule 37).

E.R.P.B.
A name consisting of initials is entered in direct order (rule 38).

Drunken Barnaby
A name consisting of a phrase which does not include a surname is entered in direct order (rule 39). This includes a name which consists of a forename and a word that is neither a title or a term of address.

Note that one of the other provisions of rule 39 caters for a name which consists of a phrase which *does* contain a surname (rule 39B). Thus Mrs. Craik (see frames 106 and 126) would be entered as:

Craik, *Mrs.*

Proceed to frame 116.

FRAME 125

The correct answer is the heading for H.G. Wells. This is the form of name by which this author is commonly identified. Herbert George Wells is not the form of name by which Wells is usually referred to. With regard to the form H   G   Wells, a decision should be made in the first instance whether to use forenames in full. Spaces should not be left for completion at a later date.

Proceed to frame 104.

FRAME 126

The choice of heading, in each case, is as follows:

a) Sir Reginald H.S. Bacon
    If a name contains a surname, titles of nobility or terms of honour that appear with the name are to be included but terms other than these are to be omitted. Thus, for Admiral Sir Reginald H.S. Bacon, K.G.B., K.C.V.O., D.S.O., the term 'Admiral' is omitted but the 'Sir' is included.

The initials, representing awards following the name, are also omitted. (Rules 31C and 31D);

b) E.R.P.B.
When a name cannot be found in available English-language reference sources, the form of name to be used is that which appears in the chief source of information (the title page in this case) of the work (rule 31B2(b));

c) Mrs. Craik
When a name consists solely of a surname, any term which normally appears with the name is included (rule 31D, second paragraph).

If you were correct proceed to frame 107 – if wrong read through frame 106 and rule 31 again before proceeding.

FRAME 127
You would need to consult an appropriate reference source or other works and/or articles by or about Rodin (see rule 31B1(b)). In fact, Rodin is entered in reference sources both as Auguste Rodin and as Francois Auguste Rodin, but the first of these forms is the most common and would be the form chosen.
Proceed to frame 106.

FRAME 128
The answer is the heading for Mistinguett. This is the pseudonym that this performer always used and it is also the name which appears on the title page of her autobiography. Entry is, therefore, made under the pseudonym.
Proceed to frame 108.

FRAME 129
The headings are:

Coles-Mogford, Anne
Rule 34C2 instructs that hyphenated names are to be entered under the first element;

Vaughan Williams, Ralph
Rule 34C4 instructs that compound surnames are to be entered under the first element unless the person's language is Portuguese;

Plas, Michel van der

Rule 34D1 instructs that for languages other than English, French, German, Italian and Spanish, names should be entered under the part following the prefix.

If you were correct proceed to frame 113. If not, re-examine rule 34 before proceeding.

FRAME 130

The names which should be chosen as the basis for entry headings are:

> Spike Milligan
> Pancho Gonzales
and   Joseph Conrad

These are the forms of name which appear in the chief sources of information of works written by these authors. You will note that they are also the names by which these people are commonly known.

Proceed to frame 105.

FRAME 131

Rules 45 to 47 of the *Concise AACR2* deal with 'Geographic names', the 'places' which frequently constitute essential elements in headings for corporate bodies. They may be required to differentiate bodies with identical names; they may be used as additions to corporate names (e.g. for conferences); and, in many instances, they are used as headings for governments.

The current English form of name, as determined first from gazetteers and atlases or, secondly, from other English-language reference sources, is the name that should be used (rule 46A).

    Austria
not   Österreich

    Japan
not   Nippon

If the name of the place is a name of a country, as in the examples above, then there is no need to add the name of a larger place. The same applies to other geographic names, such as states, provinces, territories, etc. of the United States, Canada and Australia and to the major parts of the British Isles (England, the Republic of Ireland, Northern Ireland, Scotland, Wales, etc.) (see rule 46B1), e.g.:

California
Ontario
New South Wales
England
Isle of Man

However, for geographic names other than those listed in rule 46B1, the name of the appropriate larger place in which the geographic name is located is added, using standard abbreviations when available (rule 46B2), e.g.:

Toronto *(Ont.)*
Manchester *(England)*

As in the examples above, if the first place name is being used as an entry element, the larger place is added in parentheses.

If the place name is being used as an addition, the larger place is preceded by a comma, e.g.:

Crest Hotel *(Coventry, England)*

Examine rules 45 and 46. How would these rules help you to distinguish between the city of Liverpool in Great Britain, the town of Liverpool in Nova Scotia, Canada, and the town of Liverpool in New South Wales, Australia?

Turn to frame 152 for the answers.

FRAME 132

If the name of a place changes, then the latest name is used unless the place is being referred to at a time when the earlier name was in use (rule 47). With the recent turbulent history of various countries, this rule is very pertinent. Events in the Baltic States, in the German Democratic Republic, in the USSR, in Yugoslavia, and so on, have led to a number of place-name changes.

For example, 'Rhodesia' would be used when referring to this place up to 1980, but after that date the name 'Zimbabwe' would be used.

Using any reference sources that are available to you, can you find the current name of what was, until 1980, the 'New Hebrides'?

Turn to frame 155 for the answer.

FRAME 133

Rules 48 to 56 of the *Concise AACR2* deal with headings for corporate bodies, a corporate body being an organization or group of persons that is identified by a particular name. Examples of corporate bodies include industrial or commercial organizations, such as 'Gulf Air' or 'Christian Dior'; associations and societies, such as the 'Advertising Association' or the 'Budgerigar Society';

religious bodies, such as the 'Church of England'; conferences, such as the 'International Conference on Automated Guided Vehicle Systems'; and so on.

The basic prepotent rule (rule 49A) states that, in general, entry is made under the *name* of the body as determined from

	items issued by the body in its language;
or	from reference sources;

in that order of preference, e.g.:

Advertising Association
Alder Hey Children's Hospital
Budgerigar Society
Christian Dior
Church of England
Drexel University
Gulf Air
International Conference on Automated Guided
   Vehicle Systems
Royal Anglesey Yacht Club
Royal Shakespeare Company
Washington Post
Wire Workers Union

The only exceptions are:

i) Subordinate bodies which may need to be entered under the name of a higher body, e.g.:

British Coal. *Headquarters Technical Department*

ii) A body which may need to be entered under the name of a government, e.g.:

United States. *Department of Defense*

Now decide upon the headings to be used for the Institute of Cancer Research and for the United Nations.

Turn to frame 161 for the answers.

FRAME 134

Examine rules 49A and 49B. Note that if a name contains (or consists of) initials, full stops are to be omitted or included according to the predominant usage of the body.

Now decide upon the headings to be used for the British Computer Society, the United States Capitol Historical Society and the firm T.J. Hughes.

Turn to frame 153 for the answers.

FRAME 135

When the name of a body changes, a new heading is established for publications appearing under the new name (rule 49C). This means that various items by the one body may appear under different headings, e.g.:

Liverpool Polytechnic

which, in 1992, became the

Liverpool John Moores University

In early 1992, a prospectus was issued by Manchester Polytechnic. Later in that year, your library acquired this prospectus but, by this time, Manchester Polytechnic had changed its name to Manchester Metropolitan University. Which of these two names would you choose as the heading for your catalogue entry?

Turn to frame 157 for the answer.

FRAME 136

One of the many problems associated with headings for corporate bodies is that of variant name forms (see rule 50), e.g.:

	Canadian Library Association
and	Association canadienne des bibliothèques

	Spain
and	Espana

If a body's name appears in different languages, the official English form is to be used, if there is one (rule 50A). If there is no official English form, then the form to be used is that which is in a language familiar to the users of the particular catalogue. Otherwise the name should be translated into English.

If the name is that of a government, then the conventional name, that is the geographic name, should be used (rule 50B).

Examine rules 50A and 50B, and then decide on the forms of name to be chosen from the variant names of the two bodies given above.

Turn to frame 149 for the answers.

FRAME 137

If a body uses different names in items issued by the body, the name to be used is that which appears in chief sources of information rather than forms found elsewhere (rule 50C1).

If different forms appear in the chief sources of information, then the form to be used, in this order of preference (rule 50C2), is:

> the form not linked to other words in the chief source;
> the predominant form;
> the brief form;
> the latest form.

A publication is issued by the National Railroad Passenger Corporation of America, also known as Amtrak. Both names appear on the title page, but neither form of name is given greater prominence.

Another publication is issued by the Institution of Electrical Engineers, and both this form of name and the form IEE appear on the title page. The former name is given greater prominence.

Examine rule 50C and then decide upon the forms of name which you would choose for each of the above publications.

Turn to frame 151 for the answers.

FRAME 138

Occasionally, you may find that two or more corporate bodies have the same name, and additions to the names may be needed in order to distinguish between them. This problem is dealt with in rule 51.

If the body is identified with a country, state, province, etc., rather than with a local place, the name of the country, state, province, etc. is added (rule 51B), e.g.:

> **Library Advisory Council** *(England)*
> **Library Advisory Council** *(Wales)*

In the case of all other bodies, possible additions (rule 51C) include, as appropriate:

	the name of the local place in which the body is located;
or	the institution in which the body is located;
or	the year of founding or the years of the body's existence;
or	any other appropriate word or phrase in English.

Examples are:

> **Crest Hotel** *(Coventry, England)*
> **Crest Hotel** *(Derby, England)*
> **Crest Hotel** *(Liverpool, England)*
> **Queen's** *(Club)*
> **Queen's** *(Hotel)*
> **Queen's** *(Theatre)*

Note that it may be necessary to add more than one type of name, word or phrase, as in the St James' Church example in the *Concise AACR2*, e.g.:

> **Royal Court** *(Liverpool, England : Theatre)*
> **Royal Court** *(London, England : Hotel)*
> **Royal Court** *(London, England : Theatre)*

Read through rule 51, taking particular note of the illustrative examples and then attempt to distinguish between the following bodies:

a) The Labour Party of Australia and The Labour Party of New Zealand;

b) The Grand Hotel in Torquay, England and the Grand Hotel in Lincoln, England;

c) Merchant Taylors' School in Northwood, England and Merchant Taylors' School in Crosby, England;

d) St Oswald Church, which is a Church of England church in Warrington, England, and another St Oswald Church, which is also in Warrington but a Roman Catholic church.

Turn to frame 148 for the answers.

FRAME 139

A conference, congress or meeting that is identified by a name falls within the definition of a corporate body (see rule 23B2(e) and the *Concise AACR2* Glossary p. 135), and entry is under that name, as it appears in chief sources of information (rule 52A).

However, rule 52 instructs that certain adjustments (omissions and additions) are necessary. Words within the name which denote the number, frequency or year of the conference are omitted. Thus:

The 4th International Conference on Automated Guided Vehicle Systems

becomes:

International Conference on Automated Guided Vehicle Systems

The number (if there is one), the year, and the location (city or institution) are added, in parentheses, *after* the name, giving the heading:

International Conference on Automated Guided Vehicle Systems *(4th : 1986 : Chicago, Ill.)*

Read through rule 52 and formulate a heading for:

The First European Conference on New Technology held at the University of Southampton, 29 June-4 July 1992

Turn to frame 158 for the answer.

FRAME 140

One of the two exceptions to entry of a corporate body directly under its name (see frame 133 and rule 54) occurs when a subordinate body is entered under the name of a higher body of which it is part or to which it is related. This only happens when the subordinate body does not have an individualizing name or when it is a government agency to be entered under the name of the government (see rule 53).

For example, the name of the body may include the whole of the name of the higher body, e.g.:

United Nations University

which would be entered as:

United Nations. *University*

or the subordinate body may have a name that is general in nature, e.g.:

Department of Anatomy

which would be entered, as a subheading, under the name of the higher body, i.e.:

University of Edinburgh. *Department of Anatomy*

Note that, in cases of doubt, the body should be entered directly.

In the context of rule 54, how would you enter the following subordinate bodies?

a) The Trustees of the British Museum
b) The Library Association section The Association of Assistant Librarians
c) The Database Specialist Group of the British Computer Society
d) The Council of Ministers of the European Community
e) The Maritime History of Devon Project of the University of Exeter

Turn to frame 156 for the answers.

FRAME 141

The second exception to entry of a corporate body directly under name (see frame 133 and rules 53 and 55) occurs when a government body or agency is entered as a subheading under the name of a government, e.g.:

> **United States.** *Alcohol, Drug Abuse and Mental Health*
> *Administration*

If a body created and controlled by a government fits into one of the six types listed in rule 55A, then it is entered under the heading for the government. The six types are:

1 An agency whose name is general in nature;
2 An agency that has no other agency above it (for example, a ministry);
3 A legislative body;
4 A court;
5 A body that is a major armed service;
6 An embassy, consulate, etc.

Read through rule 55A, noting the illustrative examples, and then decide on the form of heading for the following government bodies:

a) The Science Museum, Great Britain
b) The United States Supreme Court
c) The Training Commission of Great Britain
d) The Commission for the Future, Australia
e) The City of Liverpool Council

Turn to frame 159 for the answers.

FRAME 142

Rule 55B deals with government officials, sovereigns, heads of state, etc.

In the case of sovereigns, presidents, heads of state, etc., the name of the government is given, followed by the name of the office, the dates of incumbency, and the brief name of the person, e.g.:

United States. *President (1989-1993 : Bush)*

Note that this is the form of heading for a president (and for a sovereign, head of state, etc.) acting in an official, governmental capacity, and *not* the heading for the person, for which rules 30–44 should be applied.

Where other government officials are concerned, the name of the government is given followed by the name of the office, eg:

Great Britain. *Prime Minister*

Examine rule 55B, and then formulate headings for Queen Victoria of Great Britain who reigned from 1837 to1901; for Georges Pompidou, President of France from 1969 to 1974; and, for the Mayor of San Francisco.

Turn to frame 150 for the answers.

FRAME 143

When a subordinate body or government agency is entered subordinately, it may be that it is part of another subordinately entered body or agency. For example, in Great Britain, the Health and Safety Commission is subordinate to the Department of Employment, which is itself subordinate to the government.

In such cases the intervening body (or bodies) is omitted *unless* the heading would not provide sufficient identification without it (or them) (rule 56A). Thus the body used as an example above would be entered as:

Great Britain. *Health and Safety Commission*

What form of heading would you use for:

a) The Australian Studies Centre, which is part of the Institute of Commonwealth Studies of the University of London;

b) The Registrar's Advisory Committee of the Public Lending Right Office of the British government?

Turn to frame 154 for the answers.

FRAME 144

If a government agency is part of a major armed service, it is entered as a sub-heading of that major armed service (rule 56B).

Examine rule 56B, and then choose the form of heading for:

a) The United States Marine Corps
b) The London Scottish Regiment, a regiment of the British Army.

Turn to frame 160 for the answers.

FRAME 145

Note that it might be necessary to use more than one rule when deciding upon a form of heading for a corporate body. Thus, several rules were used in formulating the following heading:

Liverpool. *(England). Council*

which was used as an example in frames 141 and 159.

Firstly, the Council is a legislative body created and controlled by a government – rule 55A Type 3 – and it is therefore entered as a subheading to that government. Secondly, the conventional name, i.e. the geographic name, is used as the heading for the government – rule 50B. Thirdly, the name of an appropriate larger place is added to the name of a place in accordance with rule 46B2.

Proceed to next frame.

FRAME 146

In frame 139 we considered specific rules for conferences, etc., and in frame 140, rules for subordinate bodies which do not have individualizing names. A conference can in fact be a subordinate body.

For example, consider the first annual Conference of the Association of Child Care Officers held in Manchester in 1968. The Conference is a subordinate body with a name that is general in nature and it must, therefore, be entered subordinately – rule 54:

Association of Child Care Officers. *Conference*

To this heading must be added the number, year and location – rule 52C:

Association of Child Care Officers. *Conference (lst :*
1968 : Manchester, England)

This is a further instance when it is necessary to use more than one rule in the formulation of a heading (see previous frame).

Proceed to next frame.

FRAME 147

This almost completes our study of forms of heading, but before proceeding to the next phase, let us return for a moment to the introductory rules for headings for persons and for corporate bodies (rules 30 and 48).

These rules describe the steps to be taken when making such headings.

In both cases, you should first choose the name that will be the basis for the heading.

Then, in the case of a person, you should decide which part of the chosen name should be the first word, i.e. the filing element. In the majority of instances, this is simply the surname. Lastly, you should make references from different names of the same person or from different parts of the chosen name. For example, if you were cataloguing a novel by Christine Brooke-Rose, the steps that you would take would be:

Step 1	Choose the name that will be the basis for the heading. This would be the name by which the person is commonly known – Christine Brooke-Rose (rule 31A);
Step 2	Decide which part of the name is to be the first, lead entry word. This would be the surname Brooke-Rose – rule 34A – and, because the name is hyphenated, rule 34C2 also applies, and entry is under the first element;
Step 3	Make references from different parts of the chosen name, that is from Rose (references are dealt with in a later phase – phase six).

Where corporate bodies are concerned, having chosen the name that will be the basis for the heading, you must decide whether the name needs additions to distinguish it from other names. If the body is a conference, etc., certain omissions and additions must always be made. Then, if the body is a part of another body or is an agency of government, you must decide whether the body is to be entered directly or subordinately. Lastly, you should make references from different names for the same body, or from different parts of the chosen name.

For example, you might have to catalogue a work issued by the American Central Intelligence Agency of the United States. The steps that you would take in this case would be:

Step 1	Choose the name that will be the basis for the heading, in this case the Central Intelligence Agency – rule 49A;
Step 2	Decide whether the name needs any additions to distinguish it from other names – rule 51. No additions are needed in this case;

Step 3	As this is a government agency, consideration must be given to entry under the name of the government – rule 49B. Rule 55A then tells us that this particular body *would* be entered under the name of the government, that is United States
Step 4	Make references from the different forms of name, in this case from Central Intelligence Agency to United States. (As noted above, references are dealt with in phase six). In this particular instance, as this agency is also known as the CIA, an additional reference would be needed from this form.

Proceed to phase five following frame 161.

FRAME 148
The answers are:

a) **Labour Party** *(Australia)*
   Labour Party *(New Zealand)*

b) **Grand Hotel** *(Lincoln, England)*
   Grand Hotel *(Torquay, England)*

c) **Merchant Taylors' School** *(Crosby, England)*
   Merchant Taylors' School *(Northwood, England)*

d) **St. Oswald Church** *(Warrington, England : Church of England)*
   St. Oswald Church *(Warrington, England : Catholic)*

Each of the Labour Parties is identified with a country, so the name of that country is added (rule 51B). A similar example to this is used in rule 45 of the *Concise AACR2*.

The Grand Hotels and the Merchant Taylors' Schools are not associated with the name of a country, state, province, etc., but it is appropriate to add the names of the local places in which the bodies are located (rule 51C).

The two St. Oswald Churches are located in the same place and, therefore, something more than the local place name is required. The church denomination is suitable for this purpose. Rule 51C again applies, and take note of the St. James' Church examples.

Proceed to frame 139.

FRAME 149
The answers are:

Canadian Library Association

that is, the official *English* form (see rule 50A), and:

Spain

that is, the conventional name of the government (see rule 50B) as found in current *English*-language gazetteers and atlases (see rule 46A).
Proceed to frame 137.

FRAME 150
The answers are:

> **Great Britain.** *Sovereign (1837-1901 : Victoria)*
> **France.** *President (1969-1974 : Pompidou)*
> **San Francisco** *(Calif.) Mayor*

If you were incorrect, re-examine rule 55B before proceeding to frame 143.

FRAME 151
The correct forms of name are:

Amtrak

and

Institution of Electrical Engineers

In the first instance, as neither name is given greater prominence, the brief form is the form chosen – rule 50C2(c).
Where the Institution of Electrical Engineers is concerned, this is the form which is given greater prominence – rule 50C2(b).
Note that references would be required from the other forms of name (see phase six).
Proceed to frame 138.

FRAME 152

The places would be distinguished as follows:

Liverpool *(England)*
Liverpool *(N.S.)*
Liverpool *(N.S.W.)*

If a place is located in England, then England is added (rule 46B2). If a place is in a state, etc. of Canada or Australia, the name of the state, etc. is added (46B2), using standard abbreviations as appropriate.

Proceed to frame 132.

FRAME 153

All three of these bodies should be entered directly under their names, i.e.:

British Computer Society
United States Capitol Historical Society
T.J. Hughes

The first two bodies are *not* government bodies, so that entries such as

Great Britain. *Computer Society*

and

Washington. *United States Capitol Historical Society*

would be completely wrong. The first of these incorrect entries, in any case, distorts the name, and this pitfall should be avoided.

Entering T.J. Hughes under

Hughes, T.J.

would also distort the name. This is a firm, not a personal name, and the heading should not be inverted. The name contains initials and full stops should be included or omitted according to the predominant usage of the body. The name is usually presented as shown with full stops included.

Note that references would be required from forms of name not used (see phase six).

Proceed to frame 135.

FRAME 154

The answers are:

a) **University of London.** *Australian Studies Centre*

The intervening body is not required for the purposes of identification;

b) **Great Britain.** *Public Lending Right Office. Registrar's Advisory Committee*

In this case, the name of the committee does not provide sufficient identification without the Public Lending Right Office, which is itself subordinate to the government.

Note that references would be required from forms of name not used (see phase six).

Proceed to frame 144.

FRAME 155

The answer is Vanuatu. Note that cataloguers must have access to a wide variety of reference sources.

Proceed to frame 133.

FRAME 156

The subordinate bodies would be entered as follows:

a) **British Museum.** *Trustees*
b) **Association of Assistant Librarians**
c) **British Computer Society.** *Database Specialist Group*
d) **European Community.** *Council of Ministers*
e) **Maritime History of Devon Project**

Trustees, Database Specialist Group and Council of Ministers are all names which do not individualize these subordinate bodies, unlike the names Association of Assistant Librarians and the Maritime History of Devon Project. It is clear that the latter two names can 'stand alone', whilst the other three cannot.

Note that references would be required, as necessary, from forms of name not used (see phase six).

Proceed to frame 141.

FRAME 157

The work should be entered under the name which was in use at the time of publication (see rule 49C), i.e.:

Manchester Polytechnic

References would link the old and new names.
Proceed to frame 136.

FRAME 158

The heading would be:

European Conference on New Technology *(1st : 1992 :*
University of Southampton)

The number is omitted from the beginning of the name, but added after it, together with the year and the location, which, in this instance, is the institution.

Look again at the examples included in rule 52, and then proceed to frame 140.

FRAME 159

The answers are:

a) **Science Museum**
This body does not belong to any of the types listed in rule 55A and is, therefore, entered directly;

b) **United States.** *Supreme Court*
This body, being a court, comes within rule 55A Type 4 and is entered under the name of the government;

c) **Great Britain.** *Training Commission*

d) **Australia.** *Commission for the Future*

e) **Liverpool.** *(England). Council*
All three of these bodies have names which are general in nature (rule 55A Type 1), and so they are entered under the names of the respective governments.

Note that references would be required, as necessary, from forms of name not used (see phase six).
Proceed to frame 142.

FRAME 160

The form of headings are:

a) **United States.** *Marine Corps*

The Marine Corps is a major armed service and is entered under the heading for the government – rule 55A Type 5;

b) **Great Britain.** *Army. London Scottish Regiment*

The London Scottish Regiment is part of a major armed service and is therefore entered as a subheading to that service.

Note that references would be required, as necessary, from forms of name not used (see phase six).

If you were incorrect, examine rules 55A Type 5 and 56B once again, before proceeding to frame 145.

FRAME 161

The answer, in each case, is that entry should be made directly under name in accordance with rule 49B, i.e.:

> **Institute of Cancer Research**
> **United Nations**

Proceed to frame 134.

UNIFORM TITLES

Concise AACR2 Rules 57–61

FRAME 162

Some works are published under varying titles. Lewis Carroll's *Alice's adventures in Wonderland* has been published under a number of different titles. One of them, *Alice in Wonderland*, has become a more familiar title than the original. Balzac's *Le Père Goriot* has been variously translated into English as *Goriot, Father Goriot* and *Old father Goriot*. Beethoven's *Piano sonata no. 14* is also titled *Moonlight sonata*. The *Bible* is also known as *Holy Bible* and by the names of its parts the *Old* and *New testaments*.

It is obviously helpful to choose one title as the single point at which all variations of the same work may be found in a catalogue. A uniform title is, therefore, a title that brings together entries for different publications of the same work, when these publications have different titles proper.

The relevant section of *Concise AACR2* is contained in rules 57–61. It should be stressed that the use of uniform titles is *optional* (see rule 57A) and the need for them will vary from catalogue to catalogue and from work to work.

The uniform title, when used, is placed between the name heading and the title proper and is enclosed in square brackets, e.g.:

> **Carroll, Lewis**
> [Alice in Wonderland]
> Alice's adventures in Wonderland

If there is no name heading, the uniform title is given as the heading, omitting the square brackets, e.g.:

> **Bible**
> The Holy Bible

Read through rule 57, and then proceed to next frame.

FRAME 163

Uniform titles should be used when:

1) Two or more publications of the same work have different titles;
2) The publication being catalogued has a title that is unlikely to be looked for by catalogue users;
3) The item being catalogued is an ancient work or a sacred scripture;
4) The item being catalogued is a collection of, or selections from, the works of a person.

Read through the general rule 58, noting that uniform titles are not to be used for revisions of works (rule 58B), and then decide which of the following items would justify the use of a uniform title:

a) *Alice through the looking glass* : an adaptation of Lewis Carroll's *Through the looking glass*
b) *The story of Robinson Crusoe* : an abridgment of Daniel Defoe's *Robinson Crusoe*
c) *The personal computer guide* : a revised edition of *The microcomputer guide*

Turn to Frame 169 for the answers.

FRAME 164

If a uniform title is used, the title chosen is that by which the work is best known. This is decided by consulting reference sources and other publications of the same work. If in doubt, the earliest title is used (see rule 59A). The title in the original language is chosen as the uniform title, unless the work being catalogued is an older work originally written in a non-Roman alphabet (see rules 59B and 59C).

Now choose a uniform title for:

a) The William Makepeace Thackeray novel *The history of Henry Esmond, Esq, Colonel in the service of Her Majesty Queen Anne*, a work now familiarly known as *Henry Esmond*;
b) Nevil Shute's *Schach dem Schicksall*, the German version of *The chequer board*.

Turn to frame 171 for the answers.

FRAME 165

For older works written in a non-Roman alphabet (Greek, Arabic, etc.), the title by which the work is best known in English language reference sources is used as the uniform title, e.g.:

> **Aristotle**
> [Ethics]
> Aristotelis ethica Nicomachea

Read through rule 59C, and then choose a uniform title for Aristotle's *De arte poetica liber*. In your answer, use a layout similar to the other Aristotle example given above.

Turn to frame 168 for the answer.

FRAME 166

The uniform title 'Bible' is used for the *Bible* and any of its parts. In cataloguing a part of the *Bible*, add 'N.T.' or 'O.T.' and, if appropriate, the name of the part. For sacred scriptures other than the *Bible*, use the form of title found in English reference sources.

Examine rule 59D, and then choose a uniform title for:

a) *The Gospel according to St Luke*
b) *The Jewish sacred scriptures*

Turn to frame 172 for the answers.

FRAME 167

Rule 60 deals with collective titles, that is:

1) the complete works of a person;
2) selected works, or extracts from works, in more than one form by the same person; and
3) collections of all the works in one form by one person.

The uniform titles to be used in each of these cases are:

1) [Works]
2) [Selections]
3) [Essays] or [Novels] or [Plays] or [Songs] etc.

Carefully read through rule 60, and then choose a uniform title for each of the following items:

a) *The complete poems of John Keats*
b) *The complete works of Oscar Wilde : stories, plays, poems, essays*
c) *Selected poems and prose writings of John Milton*

Use the correct uniform title entry layout in your answers.

Turn to frame 170 for the answers.

FRAME 168

It should have been relatively easy to discover that the title by which this work is best known is *Poetics*, and the answer is, therefore:

Aristotle
[Poetics]
De arte poetica liber

Proceed to frame 166.

FRAME 169

Uniform titles would be required for the first two titles in accordance with rule 58A but not for the third title. Uniform titles are not used for revisions of works, even when these revisions have different titles.

Proceed to frame 164.

FRAME 170

a) An appropriate uniform title in English is used for a collection of all the works in one form by one person (rule 60C). The answer is, therefore:

> **Keats, John**
> [Poems]
> The complete poems of John Keats

b) The uniform title 'Works' is used for the complete works of a person (rule 60A). Thus the answer is:

> **Wilde, Oscar**
> [Works]
> The complete works of Oscar Wilde : stories, plays, poems, essays

c) For selected works, or extracts of works, in more than one form by the same person, the uniform title 'Selections' is used (rule 60B). This last answer is, therefore:

> **Milton, John**
> [Selections]
> Selected poems and prose writings of John Milton

This completes our study of uniform titles but before proceeding to Phase Six, following frame 172, examine rule 61 which deals with requirements for added entries and references.

FRAME 171

a) Where this item is concerned, the later title, *Henry Esmond*, is the better known and this should be chosen as the uniform title. Therefore, the uniform title entry would look like this:

> **Thackeray, William Makepeace**
> [Henry Esmond]
> The history of Henry Esmond, Esq., Colonel in the service of
> Her Majesty Queen Anne

(b) For this item, the uniform title that would be chosen is the original English title, *The chequer board*. The answer is, therefore:

Shute, Nevil
[The chequer board]
Schach dem Shicksall

If you were right proceed to frame 165. If wrong, re-examine rule 59, taking note of the various examples before proceeding.

FRAME 172
The uniform titles are:

a) **Bible. N.T. Luke**
For the *Bible*, 'O.T.' or 'N.T.' is added when necessary and, if appropriate, the name of the part;

b) **Talmud**
The *Talmud* is the form of title found in English language reference sources for *The Jewish sacred scriptures*.

Proceed to frame 167.

REFERENCES

Concise AACR2 Rules 62-65

Rules in the preceding sections of the *Concise AACR2* occasionally indicate particular types of references that are to be made in specific circumstances (see, for instance, rule 32A1).

FRAME 173

Having decided upon the form that headings chosen as access points will take, in accordance with rules 30 to 61, alternative forms of these headings must be considered.

Rule 62A directs that a 'see' reference must be made from a variant name or form of name of a person *or* corporate body *or* work, to the form of name that has been chosen as the name heading or uniform title heading.

For example, as Jeanne Bourgeois is to be entered under her pseudonym, Mistinguett (see frames 107 and 128), a reference is required from the form not used:

Bourgeois, Jeanne
see **Mistinguett**

Similarly, for the corporate heading Institution of Electrical Engineers (see frames 137 and 151) a reference is needed, as follows:

IEE
see **Institution of Electrical Engineers**

Read through rules 62A, 63A1 and 63A2, and then formulate a reference from the alternative form of the heading:

Brooke-Rose, Christine

(see frame 147).

Turn to frame 186 for the answer.

FRAME 174

The 'see' reference acts as a 'signpost', which simply says to the catalogue user: 'You are going the wrong way, there is no information here, proceed via ... where information *will* be found', e.g.:

United Nations. *World Health Organisation*
see **World Health Organisation**

Read through rule 64A and then formulate a 'see' reference for the United States Central Intelligence Agency (see frame 147).

Turn to frame 188 for the answer.

FRAME 175

Another type of reference, the 'see also' reference, says to the catalogue user: 'Yes, there is some information here but you should also try ... where further related information may be found', e.g.:

Amis, *Sir* **Kingsley**
see also **Markham, Robert**

The above reference links the works of one person which are entered under two different headings (see rule 63B, and frames 108 and 122). A similar reference may be made when two corporate bodies are related but entered independently (see rule 64B), e.g.:

British Iron and Steel Federation
see also **Iron and Steel Institute**

It should be obvious that, in these instances, a reference in the reverse direction will also be required, i.e.:

Markham, Robert
see also **Amis,** *Sir* **Kingsley**

Iron and Steel Institute
see also **British Iron and Steel Association**

It is possible that a reference may need to be made to more than one heading, e.g.:

Cooper, Dorothy
see also
Castillo, Carmen
Mason, Margaret
Newland, Jill
Saville, Shirley

In this instance, an author has written under her real name and several pseudonyms. It will, of course, be necessary to make similar references under the other headings. Make such a reference from the first of the listed pseudonyms.

Turn to frame 184 for the answer.

FRAME 176

Evan Hunter writes under his real name and under his pseudonym, Ed McBain. How would these two names be linked by means of references?

Turn to frame 189 for the answer.

FRAME 177

Where headings for persons are concerned, here are some illustrative examples of occasions when it will be necessary to make 'see' references:

a) Different names, for example, real name and pseudonym, e.g.:

> **Barber, Margaret Fairless**
> *see* **Fairless, Michael**

b) Different forms of name, e.g.:

> **Lawrence, David Herbert**
> *see* **Lawrence, D.H. (David Herbert)**

c) Different entry elements, e.g.:

> **Roche, Mazo de la**
> *see* **De La Roche, Mazo**

The relevant rules, which should be re-examined, are 63A1 and 63A2.

Nevil Shute Norway wrote under the pen-name Nevil Shute. The latter name was used as an example in frame 164. Formulate the reference which would be required in this instance.

Turn to frame 183 for the answer.

FRAME 178

'See' references are made from alternative names of corporate bodies in such instances as:

a) Different names, e.g.:

> **Quakers**
> *see* **Society of Friends**

b) Different forms of name, e.g.:

> **Roman Catholic Church**
> *see* **Catholic Church**

c) Different forms of heading, e.g.:

> **United States.** *Tennesseee Valley Authority*
> *see* **Tennessee Valley Authority**

The relevant rules are 64A1 and 64A2. After examining these rules, answer the following question. If the filing convention used in your catalogue files initials with full stops (periods) differently from those without full stops, is it necessary to refer from the form with full stops to the form without full stops, e.g.: from I.E.E. to IEE?

Turn to frame 185 for the answer.

FRAME 179

When 'see also' references are made between independently entered but related bodies, the relationship may be explained where necessary (see rule 64B), e.g.:

Liverpool Polytechnic
see also the later heading
Liverpool John Moores University

Make a reverse reference from the later name.
Turn to frame 182 for the answer.

FRAME 180

In certain instances, a 'see' reference is also made from a 'name-title' (the name heading and title proper of an item), or from a title, as directed in rule 65A. For example, here is a reference from a name heading and title proper to a name heading and uniform title of a work (see frame 165 and rule 65A1):

Aristotle
Aristotelis ethica Nicomachea
see **Aristotle**
Ethics

Read through rule 65A. In rule 65A2, note the Lewis Carroll example and refer to frame 162 where this item was cited to illustrate the use of a uniform title. In rule 65A4, note the *Pentateuch* example. Formulate a similar reference for *The Gospel according to St Luke*, which was used as an example in frame 172.
Turn to frame 187 for the answer.

FRAME 181

This almost completes our study of references, except to note that where titles are concerned, 'see also' references are also made to connect related works.
Examine rule 65B before proceeding to phase seven, following frame 189.

FRAME 182
The answer is:

> **Liverpool John Moores University**
> *see also the earlier name*
> **Liverpool Polytechnic**

Examine the Screen Workers' Guild example in rule 64B.
   Proceed to frame 180.

FRAME 183
The reference would be:

> **Norway, Nevil Shute**
> *see* **Shute, Nevil**

Examine the 'real name to pseudonym' examples in rule 63A1.
   Proceed to frame 178.

FRAME 184
The answer is:

> **Castillo, Carmen**
> *see also*
> **Cooper, Dorothy**
> **Mason, Margaret**
> **Newland, Jill**
> **Saville, Shirley**

   If you were incorrect, examine rule 63B again before proceeding to frame 176.

FRAME 185
Yes, a reference would be required (see the Unesco example in rule 64A1). In this instance, the reference would not be from I.E.E. to IEE, but from I.E.E. to the chosen heading, i.e. the full form of name (see also frame 173):

> **I.E.E.**
> *see* **Institution of Electrical Engineers**

It is obviously more efficient to refer directly to the heading which is in use rather than to an intermediate heading.
   Proceed to frame 179.

FRAME 186

It is possible that a catalogue user might search for Christine Brooke-Rose under the name Rose. As Brooke-Rose has been chosen as the form of heading, a reference must be made from the other form. The answer is, therefore:

> **Rose, Christine Brooke-**
> *see* **Brooke-Rose, Christine**

See also the Sackville-West example in rule 63A2 at the top of page 125 of the *Concise AACR2* (but note that there is a typographical error, in that the hyphen has been omitted from the end of Sackville – refer to rule 26.2A3 of the full *AACR2* for confirmation).

Proceed to frame 174.

FRAME 187

The reference would be:

> **Luke**
> *see*
> **Bible.   N.T.   Luke**

Note that the other references which would be required, in this instance, are:

> **Holy Bible**
> *see* **Bible**

> **New Testament**
> *see* **Bible.   N.T.**

These two references would obviously serve for all New Testaments and/or Bibles in the catalogue.

Have another look at rules 59D and 65A4, making sure that you understand the reasons for these references, before proceeding to frame 181.

FRAME 188

The answer is:

> **Central Intelligence Agency**
> *see* **United States.** *Central Intelligence Agency*

This is an example of a reference from an alternative form of heading when entry has been made as a subheading under the name of a higher body (see rules 54 and 55A). Such a reference is not specifically provided for in rule 64, but falls within the general rule, i.e. 'refer from a form of name ... if it differs from that used in the heading for the body' (rule 64A1).

A similar reference would be required from the alternative form of name, CIA.

Proceed to frame 175.

FRAME 189

The names would be linked by 'see also' references in either direction, i.e.:

> **Hunter, Evan**
> *see also* **McBain, Ed**
>
> **McBain, Ed**
> *see also* **Hunter, Evan**

See also the J.I.M. Stewart/Michael Innes example in rule 63B.
Proceed to frame 177.

ANALYTICAL ADDED ENTRIES

Concise AACR2 Rule 29B8

FRAME 190

An analytical entry is an entry for a separate *part* of a larger entity. The 'part' might be a separately titled section of a work or a separate work contained in a collection. One example might be the text of a play within a collection of plays and another example might be one musical composition from a sound recording containing a number of compositions.

It is impossible to legislate as to what will or will not be done, with regard to analytical entries, by a particular library or cataloguing agency. Policies will differ and may well be influenced by limitations of staff or finance or by some other constraint. The *Concise AACR2* recognizes this and simply states that analytical entries should be made as required by the particular library.

Proceed to next frame.

FRAME 191

The *Concise AACR2* describes two methods of making analytical entries:

a) Name–title added entries;
b) 'In' entries.

For example, *The story of the inexperienced ghost* by H.G. Wells is contained in *The first Armada ghost book*. Analytical entries for this part, formulated using each of the above methods, are as follows:

a) **Wells, H.G.**
    The story of the inexperienced ghost
    The First Armada ghost book / edited by Christine Bernard. —
    London : Armada, 1967. — 158 p. ; 18 cm. — Contains eleven ghost stories for children

b) **Wells, H.G.**
    The story of the inexperienced ghost / H.G. Wells. — p. 47-65 ;
    18 cm.
    In The First Armada ghost book / edited by Christine Bernard. —
    London : Armada, 1967

As can be seen, the first method uses the name/title (or the title) of the part as an added entry heading. The entry for the item as a whole is given below this heading.

The second method may be used if more detail relating to the part is required. In the above example, the additional detail includes the pages upon which the part appears and the size of the part. Details of the whole item are given following the word *In*.

These methods are explained in rule 29B8. Read through this rule.

The work *Three adventures of the Scarlet Pimpernel* contains three stories of the Scarlet Pimpernel in the one volume. These stories are, in the order in which they appear: *The Scarlet Pimpernel* (281 p.); *The triumph of the Scarlet Pimpernel* (188 p.); and *Eldorado* (189 p.). Each story is separately paged. The book is 18 centimetres high; it was published in Leicester by Knight Books in 1974. The author is, of course, Baroness Orczy. Prepare an analytical entry for *Eldorado*, using the first of the above methods.

Turn to frame 194 for the answer.

FRAME 192

The reference would be:

> **Burton,** *Mrs* **Montague**
> *see* **Orczy, Emmuska,** *Baroness*

The *Concise AACR2* does not specifically instruct that the term of address of a married woman, identified by her husband's name, should be added, but it would seem to be necessary in a case such as this.

Proceed to next frame.

FRAME 193

On pages 132 to 146 of W.A. Munford's *Penny rate : aspects of British public library history, 1850-1950* appears a section by Joan Edmondson entitled *Mechanics' institutes and public libraries. Penny rate* was published in London by the Library Association in 1951; it contains 150 pages and is 22 centimetres high. Produce analytical entries for Edmondson's work, using each of the methods described above in frame 191.

Turn to frame 195 for the answers.

FRAME 194

The answer is:

> **Orczy, Emmuska,** *Baroness*
>   Eldorado
>   Three adventures of the Scarlet Pimpernel / Baroness
> Orczy. —   Leicester : Knight, 1974. — 281, 188, 189 p. —
> 18 cm. — Contents: The Scarlet Pimpernel — The triumph of
> the Scarlet Pimpernel — Eldorado

The author and title of the part are used as the added entry heading, followed by the entry for the item as a whole. Note the way in which the pagination is recorded, the number of pages in each sequence being given in the order in which they appear in the item (see rule 5B2). The contents note is formulated in accordance with rule 7B14.

Using the second analytical entry method and an *In* note, the entry would appear as follows:

> **Orczy, Emmuska,** *Baroness*
> Eldorado / Baroness Orczy. — 189 p. [470-658]. — 18 cm.
> *In* Orczy, Emmuska, Baroness. Three adventures of the Scarlet Pimpernel. — Leicester : Knight, 1974

This entry is reasonably straightforward (see the George Eliot example in rule 29B8b) except for the recording of the pagination of the part. The solution adopted here is to give the actual pagination followed by an indication of the position of the part in the item as a whole in square brackets.

Alert students will have noted that the form of name used here for Baroness Orczy is that actually used as an example in the *Concise AACR2* (rule 40A). However, the forename Emmuska does not usually appear in her books, nor is it always given in reference sources, and there would appear to be an argument for using the simpler form Orczy, Baroness, as the form of name by which she is commonly known.

Baroness Orczy was married to Montague Burton and a reference from this alternative name would be required. What would this reference be?

Turn to frame 192 for the answer.

FRAME 195
The analytical entries are:

> **Edmondson, Joan**
> Mechanics' institutes and public libraries
> Penny rate : aspects of British public library history, 1850-1950 / W.A. Munford. — London : Library Association, 1951. — 150 p. ; 22 cm. — Includes: Mechanics' institutes and public libraries / Joan Edmondson

> **Edmondson, Joan**
> Mechanics' institutes and public libraries. — p. 132-146. — 22 cm.
> *In* Munford, W.A. Penny rate : aspects of British public library history. — London : Library Association, 1951

Examine these answers carefully to make sure that you understand the way in which they were obtained. The contents note was formulated in accordance with rule 7B14 for an item which contains a part which is not evident from the rest of the description. The pagination upon which the part appears could have been added if required, i.e.:

> Includes: Mechanics' institutes and public libraries /
> Joan Edmondson: p. 132-146

A 'With' note (see rule 7B16) would have been equally valid in this case, i.e.:

> With: Mechanics' institutes and public libraries / Joan Edmondson

This completes our study of analytical added entries.
Proceed to phase eight which follows.

WORKED EXAMPLES

You should now be able to catalogue an item fully (apart from classification and subject work) using all of the sections and rules of the *Concise AACR2*. The frames in this phase are designed to test whether you can, in fact, do this. Following this page are the reproductions of six chief sources of information. These will be used as worked examples in the subsequent frames.

EXAMPLE 1

THE BASICS
OF DATA
MANAGEMENT FOR
INFORMATION
SERVICES

PETER G. UNDERWOOD
Professor of Librarianship, University of Cape Town
and
RICHARD J. HARTLEY
Lecturer, Department of Information and Library Studies,
University College of Wales, Aberystwyth

Library Association Publishing
London

EXAMPLE 2

First published 1982
by Richard Drew Publishing Ltd
Reprinted 1982, 1984, 1985
Second edition 1986
Reprinted 1987
Third edition 1988
Reprinted 1989 (twice),1990

This edition published 1991 by W & R Chambers Ltd,
43 – 45 Annandale Street, Edinburgh EH7 4AZ

**British Library Cataloguing in
Publication Data**

A catalogue record for this book is
available from the British Library

ISBN 0-550-22003-8

Printed and bound in Great Britain by
Cox & Wyman Ltd

THE
**GERMAN
TRAVELMATE**

compiled by
LEXUS
with
Ingrid Schumacher

Chambers

EXAMPLE 3

1. SINGIN' THE BLUES (Robinson/Conrad/Lewis Young)
2. OSTRICH WALK (Dixieland Jazz Band)
3. RIVERBOAT SHUFFLE (Voynow/Carmichael/Mills/Parish)
4. I'M COMING VIRGINIA (Heywood/Cook)
5. WAY DOWN YONDER IN NEW ORLEANS (Creamer/Layton)
6. FOR NO REASON AT ALL IN C (Trumbauer/Bix/Beiderbecke)
7. WRINGIN' AND TWISTIN' (Trumbauer/Waller/Irene)
8. THREE BLIND MICE (Trumbauer/Morehouse)
9. AT THE JAZZ BAND BALL (La Rocca/Shields)
10. ROYAL GARDEN BLUES (Williams/Williams)
11. JAZZ ME BLUES (Delaney)
12. GOOSE PIMPLES (Irwin/Henderson)
13. SORRY (Klages/Quicksell)
14. CRYIN' ALL DAY (Trumbauer/Morehouse)
15. A GOOD MAN IS HARD TO FIND (Green)
16. SINCE MY BEST GAL TURNED ME DOWN (Quicksell)
17. THERE'LL COME A TIME (WAIT AND SEE) (I. Maxwell/M. Wolf)
18. JUBILEE (Robinson)
19. OUR BUNGALOW OF DREAMS (Malie/Verges/Verges)
20. LILA (Gottler/Tobias/Pinkard)

[SPA] – MADE IN THE EEC
Country of Origin UK

Charly Records Limited
156-166 Ilderton Road, London SE15 1NT

CHARLY RECORDS

QBCD 18

The compilation
℗ 1993 Charly Records Ltd
© 1993 Charly Records Ltd

Exclusively manufactured
for Entertainment UK Ltd
by Charly Records Ltd

compact disc DIGITAL AUDIO

BIX BEIDERBECKE

Singin' The Blues

See Inlay For
Track Details

QBCD 18

compact disc DIGITAL AUDIO

The Compilation
℗ 1993 Charly Records Ltd
© 1993 Charly Records Ltd

CHARLY RECORDS

Country of Origin UK
[SPA] – MADE IN THE EEC

EXAMPLE 4

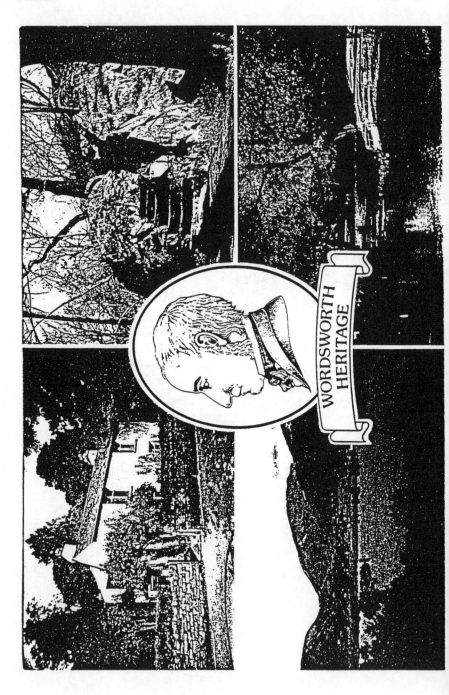

EXAMPLE 5

AS-EASY-AS Version 4.00T . . . . (C) Copyright, TRIUS,Inc 1989,90
AS-EASY-AS is Shareware. UNMODIFIED copies of the program (NOT THE MANUAL) may be distributed for a 30-day evaluation period provided that no payment, commercial benefit or other consideration is received. The program MAY NOT be combined with any software and/or hardware without prior written consent from:

All Rights Reserved Worldwide
TRIUS, Inc.
231 Sutton St, Suite 2D-3
North Andover, MA 01845 USA
Tel. (508) 794-9377

THE EXTRAORDINARY SPREADSHEET

```
 _____
|  _____    |
| | AS-EASY-AS |                   |
| |_____|  |
|_____|
```
tm

■ 8192 Rows/256 Columns   ■ Choice of 10 Graph Types   ■ X-Y Regression
■ dBIII/IV Import/Export   ■ 9/24 Pin & Laser Support   ■ Eqn Solving
■ Macro Playback   ■ Worksheet Linking   ■ Blinding Speed
■ Database Input Forms   ■ Matrix Operations   ■ Minimal Recalc
■ Math/Logic/Statistical/Financial/Date/String & User Defined Functions

```
 _____
| In the United Kingdom you may register by sending £45+£4 pp + vat to: |
| SHAREWARE PUBLISHING, 3 Queens St., SEATON, DEVON, EX12 2NY            |
| Tel. 0297 24088  - Credit Cards Purchases & Site Licensing Available!  |
|_____|
```

(Prices subject to change without notice - call for latest version/price)
< Press any key to continue >

EXAMPLE 6

Journal of Business & Finance Librarianship

Volume 1
Number 1
1990

CONTENTS

EDITOR'S INTRODUCTION   1

Finding a Job: The Complementary Roles of the Library
and Placement Office   3
     Linda F. Eichler
     Steven J. Bell

Building a Case for a Computerized Undergraduate Business
Law Library   15
     James E. Samels

A Selected Guide to Foreign Trade Statistical Sources   33
     Michael S. Gelinne

The Dow Jones News/Retrieval Service in an Academic
Library   45
     William R. Kinyon
     Katharine E. Clark

Trade Associations and New Perspective in Library Service:
A Study of the Indiana Chamber of Commerce Library   57
     John A. Kristelli

Volume 1, No. 1 1990   ISSN: 0896-3568

Journal of
BUSINESS & FINANCE LIBRARIANSHIP

Published by THE HAWORTH PRESS, Inc.

FRAME 196

Let us begin by cataloguing a reasonably straightforward printed book. Example 1 is the title page of *The basics of data management for information services*. On the verso of the title page it states that the work was 'First published 1993' and the ISBN is given as 1-85604-052-6. The book contains 119 Arabic numbered pages and is not illustrated. The height of the work is 22.5 centimetres.

Produce a full description for this item. Add to this description a main entry heading to make a complete catalogue entry and indicate the access points or other headings under which you would make added entries.

Turn to frame 205 for the answers.

FRAME 197

The title page and verso of the title page from a further book, *The German travelmate*, are reproduced in Example 2. The work contains a total of 128 pages, numbered in Arabic, and includes one black and white map. Its height is 20 centimetres.

Produce a full main entry for this second item and indicate the access points or other headings under which you would make added entries. Note the numbers of the *Concise AACR2* rules that you use.

Turn to frame 207 for the answers.

FRAME 198

Example 3 is the reproduction of the label and the inlay on the container of a 4¾ inch diameter audio compact disc. Produce a full main entry for this item. What added entries, etc., might be necessary?

Turn to frame 206 for the answers.

FRAME 199

Example 4 is a graphic item, in this case a postcard, which has been reproduced in its actual size. On the reverse of the card is the following information:

WORDSWORTH

DOVE COTTAGE   POET'S SEAT

GRASMERE   RIVER RYDAL

Photography by Phil Insley

Published by J. Arthur Dixon

The postcard is coloured. No publication date is given, but the card was available for purchase during the 1980s.

Produce a main entry for this item.

Turn to frame 204 for the answer.

FRAME 200

Reproduced in Example 5 is the title screen from a computer spreadsheet program. The program is supplied on one 3½ inch disk and is accompanied by a 362 page manual. On the title page and preliminaries of this manual, it states that As-easy-as was developed by Trius, Inc. in the United States and that exclusive publication in the UK is by Shareware. On page 13 of the manual hardware requirements are given as IBM PC or compatible with 384K RAM, Hercules, CGA or higher resolution monitor, and printer. The program provides for colour on screen.

Produce a main entry for this item for a library in the United Kingdom.

Turn to frame 208 for the answer.

FRAME 201

Reproduced in Example 6 are the front cover and title page of the first issue of a serial. The serial is illustrated and is 22 centimetres in height. On the page facing the title page, it states that the item is published quarterly by the Haworth Press, Inc., Binghamton, N.Y. and, in the publisher's subscription details that accompany the item, the date of the first issue is given as fall 1990.

Produce a full description for this serial. What would be the heading for the main entry?

Turn to frame 209 for the answers.

FRAME 202

With regard to the answers to the problems in this phase, it should be noted that the *Concise AACR2* provides for a particular library or cataloguing agency to make an individual decision in certain instances, e.g.:

1) A 'general material designation' is an *optional* inclusion following the title proper (see frame 14), e.g.:

> Singin' the blues [sound recording]
>
> As-easy-as (TM) [computer file] : the extraordinary spreadsheet

2) Paragraphing could replace punctuation (. —) for the separation of areas in the description (see frame 8), e.g.:

> **Insley, Phil**
> Wordsworth heritage / photography by Phil Insley. — J.A.
> Dixon, [ca. 198-]
> 1 postcard : col. ; 12 x 17 cm.
> Contents: Wordsworth (line drawing) — Dove Cottage — Poets
> seat — Grasmere — River Rydal

Notice the way in which paragraphing tends to make the specific material designation more prominent.

3) Different libraries may opt for varying amounts of detail to be included in the description. However, rule 0E lays down a basic minimum level.

4) There may well be other differences in individual methods. For example, one library may use lower case letters in headings, e.g.:

> **Royal Shakespeare Company**

whilst another may decide on upper case:

> **ROYAL SHAKESPEARE COMPANY**

Whatever practices are followed in a particular library, however, they should be followed *consistently*. Lack of consistency leads to a chaotic catalogue.
Proceed to frame 210.

FRAME 203
The examples included in the rule for analytical entries (29B8) are for printed texts only. However, the rule makes clear (29B8(b)) that, if relevant, the description of the part can include the extent of the item, other physical details and the dimensions. A suggested answer is therefore:

> **Ostrich** walk. — on 1 sound disc : digital ; 4 3/4 in.
> *In* Beiderbecke, Bix Singin' the blues. — London :
> Charly, p1993

The 'on' has been added to make clear that *Ostrich walk* is not a separate physical entity. A similar solution would be adopted when using the full *AACR2*.
If desired, a statement of responsibility for the part could be given, i.e.:

> **Ostrich** walk / Dixieland Jazz Band. — on 1 sound ...

However, this has been omitted in the answer given above, as it was not included in the contents note in the main entry.
Proceed to frame 199.

FRAME 204

The answer is:

Insley, Phil
Wordsworth heritage / photography by Phil Insley. — J.A.
Dixon, [ca. 198-]. — 1 postcard : col. ; 12 x 17 cm. — Contents:
Wordsworth (line drawing) — Dove Cottage — Poet's seat —
Grasmere — River Rydal

The title and statement of responsibility are recorded as given on the item.
The detail relating to the constituent portrait and pictures are given here in a
contents note but, alternatively, they could have been recorded as other title
information, i.e.:

Wordsworth heritage : Wordsworth, Dove Cottage, Poet's
seat, Grasmere, River Rydal

No place of publication is given on the item, so this element is left out (rule
4C3).

Note that, in describing materials according to the *Concise AACR2*, a basic
principle is that you describe what you have in hand. Therefore, this item
must be physically described as a 1 postcard and not as 5 pictures or pho-
tographs.

A title added entry would be required according to rule 29B5.

Proceed to frame 200.

FRAME 205

The complete catalogue entry, the *main entry*, would be:

Underwood, Peter G.
The basics of data management for information
services / Peter G. Underwood and Richard J. Hartley. —
London : Library Association, 1993. — 119 p. ; 23 cm. —
ISBN 1-85604-052-6

Added entries would be required for the second author:

Hartley, Richard J.

and for the title:

The **Basics** of data management for information services

Check your answer against that given above. Note that the title and statement
of responsibility is transcribed as given in the chief source of information (the
title page) but the capitalization is not followed (rule 1B1), and the detail relating to the authors' positions is omitted (rule 1F7). The publisher is given in
the shortest form in which it can be understood and identified (rule 4D1).

The height of a book is given to the next centimetre up, therefore 22.5 cm. = 23 cm. (rule 5D(1)). The ISBN is included (rule 8B1).

When a work is by two people, and no one person is clearly principally responsible, entry is under the heading for the one named first (see rules 25B and 25C). Added entries would be required under the second person (see rule 29B1) and under the title (29B5).

Proceed to frame 197.

FRAME 206

The complete catalogue main entry for the sound recording would be:

Beiderbecke, Bix
Singin' the blues / Bix Beiderbecke. — London : Charly, p1993. — 1 sound disc : digital ; 4 3/4 in. — Contents: Singin' the blues — Ostrich walk — Riverboat shuffle — I'm coming Virginia — Way down yonder in New Orleans — For no reason at all in C — Wringin' and twistin' — Three blind mice — At the jazz band ball — Royal garden blues — Jazz me blues — Goose pimples — Sorry — Cryin' all day — A good man is hard to find — Since my best gal turned me down — There'll come a time (wait and see) — Jubilee — Our bungalow of dreams — Lila

Note that the date given is the phonogram (copyright) date, i.e. p1993 (see rule 4E2). In this instance, both a 'p' date and a 'c' date are included on the item. The latest of these dates would normally be given in the entry but, in this case, both dates are the same. A compact disc is described as 'digital', but the number of sound channels is not readily available so this information is omitted (see rule 5C(6)). The contents note would be included in the entry if the policy of the particular library or cataloguing agency required it (rule 7B14). Although the *Concise AACR2* does not instruct that the publisher's number should be given in the entry, this information may well be a useful inclusion. The number usually consists of an alphabetic and/or numeric symbol and, in accordance with the full *AACR2*, it would be preceded by the brand name or trade name associated with it, e.g.:

Charly: QBCD 18.

The number would appear at the end of the above entry, following the contents note, preceded by the standard punctuation (. —).

A sound recording of works by different persons, performed by a principal performer, is entered under the heading for that performer (rule 27B1(g)). A reference would be required (see rule 63A) from Beiderbecke's real name (Leon Bismark Beiderbecke). An added entry would be made under the title (rule 29B5) and, if required by the policy of the library or cataloguing agency, analytical added entries could be made for each separately titled work (see rule 29B8).

Assuming that a contents note had been made as shown above, produce an 'In' title analytical entry for *Ostrich walk*.

Turn to frame 203 for the answer.

FRAME 207

The complete catalogue entry, the *main entry*, would be:

> The **German** travelmate / compiled by Lexus, with Ingrid
> Schumacher. — [New] ed. — Edinburgh : Chambers, 1991. —
> 128 p. ; 16 cm. — First published by R. Drew, 1982. —
> ISBN 0-550-22003-8

Added entries would be necessary for the compilers:

> **Lexus**
> **Schumacher, Ingrid**

The title and statement of responsibility are recorded as given on the title page, except for capitalization and punctuation (title proper – rule 1B1; statement of responsibility – rule 1F1). The edition statement is given as found in the item but words are replaced by standard abbreviations (rule 2B). However, in this instance 'This edition' is clearly a 'New' edition and can be cited as such. The 'New' is enclosed in square brackets in accordance with rule 2A2 as it has not been taken from any formal statement made by the publisher. The place of publication and publisher are recorded as instructed in rules 4C1 and 4D1.   The publication date is the year of the edition (rule 4E1). The physical description includes the extent, i.e. the number of pages (rule 5B2), and the dimensions, i.e. the height to the nearest centimetre (rule 5D(1)). The work contains only one illustration and this has been ignored, since to give 'ill.' would be somewhat misleading. (The full *AACR2* would provide the solution: '128 p. : 1 map ; 16 cm.'). The note on the item's publication history is made according to rule 7B8. The standard number is given (rule 8B1).

This is a work of shared responsibility between a corporate body, Lexus (you should have appreciated that this was a corporate body from the form of name given on the verso of the title page, i.e. 'Lexus Ltd'), and a person, Ingrid Schumacher. Principal responsibility is attributed to Lexus by both typography and wording. Thus Rule 25B1 applies but, as the work then emanates from a corporate body and does not fall within any of the categories listed in rule 23B2, main entry is under title. Added entries would be required under Lexus and Schumacher according to rules 29A2 and 29B2(b). The forms of heading for the added entries are derived according to rules 49A, 49B, 31A, 31B1 and 34A.

The edition statement is given as found in the item but words are replaced by standard abbreviations (rule 2B). However, in this instance 'This edition' is clearly a 'New' edition and can be cited as such. The 'New' is enclosed in square brackets in accordance with rule 2A2 as it has not been taken from any formal statement made by the publisher.

This was not a very easy item to catalogue, especially in relation to the choice of main entry heading. If your entries were correct, proceed to frame 198, but if they were not correct, examine the entries produced above and check them against the rules indicated. Proceed only when you are certain that you understand the way in which the entries have been formulated.

FRAME 208
The answer is:

> **As-easy-as** (TM) : the extraordinary spreadsheet / Trius,
>   Inc. — Version 4.00. — Computer program. — North
> Andover : Trius ; Seaton : Shareware, 1990. — 1 computer
> disk : col. ; 3 1/2 in. + 1 manual. — System requirements:
> IBM PC or compatible; 384K RAM; Hercules or CGA or
> higher resolution monitor; printer

Note the use of the special area to indicate that this is a 'Computer program' (see rule 3B), and the inclusion of the version as the edition statement. When there are two or more publishers, optionally, the publisher in the home country can also be given (see rule 4B2). Information for this area can be taken not only from the chief source but also from any formal statement in material accompanying the item, in this case the manual (see rule 4A2). The manual is recorded as accompanying material at the end of the physical description. Where a computer file is concerned, the system requirements should *always* be given in a note (see rule 7B1).

Main entry would not be under the responsible corporate body, as it does not fall within one of the categories listed in rule 23B2. However, an added entry would be made under Trius, Inc (rule 29B2(e)), i.e.:

Trius

Proceed to frame 201.

The full description for the serial is:

> Journal of business and finance librarianship. — Vol. 1,
> no. 1 (fall 1990)-   . — Binghamton, N.Y. : Haworth,
> 1990-   . —   v. : ill. ; 22 cm. — Quarterly. — ISSN
> 0896-3568

Note the use of the special area for serials (rule 3A). The chief source of information for a printed serial is the title page of the first issue (rule 0A), but if the necessary information cannot be found in the chief source, as in this case, it may be taken from elsewhere in the item or from any source that accompanies the item and that was issued by the publisher. The addition of 'N.Y.' to the place of publication is made by analogy with the 'Burbank, Calif.' example in rule 4B2. This seems a useful addition when the catalogue user may not be aware of the location of a particular place. The publisher is given in the shortest form in which it may be understood and identified, and therefore 'Haworth Press, Inc.' is given as 'Haworth'. The date of publication is that of the first issue, and this should be followed by a hyphen and four spaces to indicate a 'live' serial (compare with the special area above, although the full *AACR* actually stipulates this (rule 12.4F1), unlike the *Concise*). The specific material designation for a 'live' printed serial is 'v.' preceded by three spaces (rule 5B4). The frequency is an important note (rule 7B1) and the ISSN should be given (rule 8B1).

The main entry would be under title, i.e. the first words of the description, according to rule 23C, e.g.:

> **Journal** of business and finance librarianship. — Vol. 1,
> no. 1 (fall 1990)-   . — Binghamton, N.Y. : Haworth,
> 1990-   . —   v. : ill. ; 22 cm. — Quarterly. — ISSN
> 0896-3568

One of the problems involved in the cataloguing of serials is that, usually, the cataloguer has to try to describe an *incomplete* item. In addition, it may well be that a library begins to subscribe to a serial some time after it began publication. The chief source of information then becomes the chief source of the first available issue (rule 0A) and very often reference sources have to be consulted in order to ascertain when publication began. The serial is always described in terms of the first issue onwards but, if a library begins to subscribe with a later issue, a library's holdings note is made (see rule 7B15), e.g.:

> Library has 1987 to date

Proceed to frame 202

FINAL NOTE

This completes our study of the *Concise AACR2*. If you have worked through this program assiduously, you should now have a sound knowledge from which to progress, so that, with more practice, you should be able to make very good use of this code of cataloguing rules. *AACR2* is arguably the best such code ever produced. The *Concise AACR2* conveys the essence of the full set of rules and follows the same basic principles.

You may have noticed that the frames with informational content in this program are arranged consecutively within each phase, so that, if it becomes necessary for you to revise certain sections, these frames may be read in sequence simply by omitting to answer the set questions. The index will assist in the location of frames dealing with specific problems.

Appendix One, which follows, contains some further illustrative examples of the cataloguing of various media.

ILLUSTRATIVE EXAMPLES

A selection of annotated examples for various media are presented here.

For those readers who wish to compare the results obtained using the *Concise AACR2* with those obtained using the full rules, these are amended examples taken from *Examples illustrating AACR2 1988 revision* / Eric J. Hunter. — Library Association, 1989.

Kits

An **Introduction** to building societies : the Halifax
   project / Halifax Building Society. — [New ed.]. —
Halifax : Halifax B.S., [1987]. — various pieces ; in
portable container 44 x 46 x 9 cm. — Includes teacher's
handbook and a computer disk containing game:
Moneymarket (system requirements: BBC B or B+). —
Designed for use in mixed-ability situations and can be
adopted to suit a variety of learning situations with
11-16 year olds

Notes Item has no main component and a large number of different materials,
therefore 'various pieces' given (rule 10C2). Container named and dimensions
given by analogy with rule 5D. Note is included describing important accompanying material (rule 7B10). Note on intended audience (rule 7B11).

Printed monographs

Abrahams, Gerald
   Trade unions & the law / by Gerald Abrahams. —
London : Cassell, 1968. — 254 p. ; 22 cm. — ISBN
0-304-91599-8

Notes Title transcribed from item exactly as found in the chief source of
information except for capitalization and punctuation (rule 1B1). Standard
number given (rule 8B1).

Maps

Hellas = Greece : map. — Scale 1:1,500,000. —
   [Greece] : N. & K. Gouvoussis, [198-]. — 1 map :
col. ; 55 x 77 cm. folded to 19 x 12 cm.

Notes Parallel title (rule 1D). Scale given as representative fraction, if it is
found on the item or can be determined easily. No instruction in *Concise
AACR2* to use 'folded to...' but full rules do give authority for this.

Music

Rodgers, Richard
   A selection of Rodgers & Hart songs / music
by Richard Rodgers ; lyrics by Lorenz Hart ;
arranged for symphonic band by Erik Leidzen. —
Conductor's condensed score. — New York :
Chappell, c1948. —   1 score ; 31 cm.

Notes Musical presentation statement included (rule 3D2). Copyright date given (rule 4E2).

Sound recordings

Sullivan, *Sir* Arthur
Patience. — London : London, p1961. — 2 sound discs : digital, stereo. ; 4 3/4 in. — Music by Sir Arthur Sullivan ; words by W.S. Gilbert ; D'Oyly Carte Opera Company and the New Symphony Orchestra of London, Isidore Godfrey, conductor. — London: 414429-2

Notes As a statement of responsibility does not appear in the chief source of information, such a statement is not given (rule 1F4). Persons and bodies not named in a statement of responsibility can, however, be given in a note (rule 7B6). Term 'digital' used for compact discs (rule 5C).

Motion pictures and videorecordings

Introducing information. — 1987. — 1 videocassette (18 min.) : sd., col. — BBC 2 television programme: Information world, broadcast on 29 Apr. 1987, presenter: Carol Leader. — VHS. — Summary: The nature of information and the use made of the computer by public libraries

Notes Videorecording from live broadcast therefore no publication details (rule 4C3). Duration given (rule 5C(5)). Note of important physical detail, i.e. VHS (rule 7B9), included. Summary if required (rule 7B13).

Graphics

Walters, Samuel
New Brighton packet / Samuel Walters. — 1835. — 1 art original : col. ; 47 x 68 cm.

Notes No place of publication or publisher for item (rule 4C3). Term 'Art original' used (rule 5B1(a)).

Computer files

Fellows, Paul
Database / Paul Fellows. — Computer program. — Cambridge : Acornsoft, 1984. — 1 computer disk : col. ; 5 1/4 in. + 1 user manual. — (Acornsoft business). — System requirements: BBC B; 40 or 80 track disk drive

Notes Computer file designation (3B2). Accompanying material given (rule 5E2). System requirements noted (rule 7B1).

Three-dimensional objects

Potter, Beatrix
A jig-saw puzzle of Jemima Puddleduck : Beatrix
Potter's famous character. — London : Warne, [ca.
197-]. — 1 jigsaw puzzle : wood, col. ; in box
22 x 22 x 4 cm.

Notes Appropriate term used for object (rule 5B1(k)). Material of which object is made given (rule 5C(7)). Container named with dimensions (rule 5D(9)).

Serials

American libraries : bulletin of the American
Library Association. — Vol. 1, no. 1 (Jan. 1970)-   . —
Chicago : ALA, 1970-   . —   v. : ill. (some col.) ; 28
cm. — Monthly, except bi-monthly Jul./Aug. — Continues:
ALA bulletin

Notes Designation and date of first issue given (rule 3A2 and 3). Extent of incomplete serial given as 'v.' preceded by three spaces (rule 5B4). Frequency note (7B1).

INDEX

Unless otherwise stated, numbers refer to frames. When a topic is dealt with in a sequence of frames, only the first relevant number will normally be given.

abbreviations
  edition statement 16
  geographic names 131
  physical description 19, 41
abridgements 59
academic degrees
  omission from statement of responsibility 15
access points (*see also* headings)
  choice of *phase two, three*
accompanying material 19, 28, 29
  worked example 208
acronyms
  corporate names 134
    references 173
adaptations 59
  of graphic art works 62
added entries 44, *phase three*
  analytical entries *phase seven*
  uniform titles 170
additions
  to conference headings 139
  to corporate names 131, 138
  to geographic names 131
  to personal names 116
    distinguishing identical names 118
  to statements of responsibility 15
address, terms of *see* titles of nobility, honour, address, etc.
administrative regulations 45
alterations of musical works 59
alternative headings 98
analytical added entries *phase seven*
  worked example 206
ancient anonymous works
  title entry 45
  uniform titles 163
annotations 21
anonymous works 45, 50
approximate date 18
areas of description 2, 8
  see also names of specific areas, e.g. Notes
armed forces 141, 144
arrangements of musical works 62
art reproductions 62

art works, adaptations 62
artists
  as personal authors 45
  collaborations with writers 60
associations *see* corporate bodies
author/title added entries *see* name/title added entries
authors *see* personal authors

Bible
  title entry 45
  uniform titles 163, 166
  references 180
bibliographies, notes on 21
bi-partite treaties 65
  uniform titles 167
books *see* printed monographs
Braille, general material designation 14
brief forms of corporate names
  entry 137
  references 173
British terms of honour, added to personal names 116
business firms *see* corporate bodies

capitalization
  headings 202
  titles 12
cartographers, as personal authors 45
cartographic materials
  general material designation 14
  special area 17
change of name (*see also* variant names)
  corporate bodies 135
  geographic names 132
  persons 107
change of title 46
chiefs of state 142
children, adaptations for 59
choice of name
  corporate bodies 133
  persons 104
  places 131
chronological designation of serials
  see designation of serials

churches (*see also* corporate bodies) 138
cities, towns etc
  added to conference names 139
  added to corporate names 138
  added to geographic names 131
city councils 141
collaborations *see* mixed responsibility;
  shared responsibility
collaborators
  added entries 88
collation *see* physical description area
collections 56
  added entries 190
  of already existing works 56
  of new works 56
  of works by one person 45, 163, 167
  with or without collective title 56
collective titles (*see also* collections)
  uniform titles 167
colour, other physical details 19
commissions, reports of 45
committees, reports of 45
compact discs
  extent 19
  worked example 198
compilers (*see also* editors)
  as personal authors 45
complete works, collective uniform title 167
composers
  as personal authors 45
  collaborations with librettists 60
compound surnames 112
  nature uncertain 113
computer data and programs *see* computer
  files
computer disks, physical description 19
computer files
  file designation 17
  general material designation 14
  physical description area 19
  special area (file characteristics) 17
  worked example 200
concordances (related works) 64
conditions of authorship/responsibility 47
conferences
  as corporate bodies 45
  as subordinate bodies 146
  entry under 45
  headings 139
congresses *see* conferences
consulates 141
contents notes 21
  analytical entries 195
conventional names of governments 136,
  145
copyright dates 18, 206

corporate bodies
  added entries 87
  capitalisation of names 202
  change of name 135
  definition 45
  entry under 45
  headings for, *see* corporate headings
  references 174
  variant names 136
corporate headings 133
  additions to 138
  capitalisation 202
  change of name 135
  direct or indirect entry 133, 140
  language 136
  references 174
  variant names 136
corporate names *see* corporate bodies;
  corporate headings
councils, city 141
countries
  added to corporate names 138
  added to geographic names 131
  governments 136
courts 141
cross-references *see* references

data, computer file designations 17
date(s)
  added to conferences 139
  added to personal names 118
  of copyright 18, 206
  of publication, distribution, etc 18
  of reprints 18
description of items *phase one*
  analytical entries *phase seven*
  areas 2, 8, 9
  levels of detail 23
  punctuation 5
  sources of information 6
  worked examples *phase eight*
designation of serials 9
detail, levels of 23, 202
diameter of items 19
dimensions
  physical description 19
direct or indirect entry
  corporate bodies 133, 140
distinguishing terms
  corporate names 138
  geographic names 131
  personal names 118
distribution area *see* publication,
  distribution, etc, area
duration (playing time) 19

edition
  date of 18
  notes on 21
edition area 2, 16
edition statement 16
editorial direction, works produced under 45, 56
editors
  added entries 87
embassies 141
enterprises *see* corporate bodies
et al., use of 15
expeditions 45
explanatory references 179
extent of items 19
extracts *see* collections; selections

facsimiles, description 23
family names *see* surnames
federal governments *see* governments
file designation, computer files 17
filing convention 178
firms *see* corporate bodies
forenames
  represented by initials,
    full name given in parentheses 118
forms of heading *phase four*
  corporate bodies 101, 133
  geographic names 101, 131
  personal names 101
frequency
  of serials 9, 209

games
  description 9
general material designation 14, 202
geographic names 101, 131
  added to conference names 139
  added to corporate names 138
  additions to 131
  changes of name 132
  choice 131
  use 131
given names, entry under 115
GMD *see* general material designation
government agencies
  as corporate bodies 45
  entered subordinately 141
government officials 142
governments
  as corporate bodies 45
  conventional names 136, 145
  names of 136
  officials 142
  subordinate bodies 133, 141, 143

graphic materials
  general material designation 14
  physical description 19
  worked example 199

headings 42, *phase four*
  choice of access points *phase two*
    added entries *phase three*
  forms of heading *phase four*
    corporate bodies 101, 133
    geographic names 101, 131
    personal names 101
heads of state 142
height of item 19, 205
honour, terms of *see* titles of nobility, honour, address, etc
hyphenated names 112

identical personal names,
  addition to 118
illustrations
  physical description 19
  texts with 59, 63
illustrators, added entries 91
'in' analytical entries 191, 203
imprint *see* publication, distribution, etc., area
in-house style 8
indirect or direct entry
  corporate bodies 133, 140
initials
  corporate names 134
  entry under, persons 115
  personal names consisting of or
    containing, additions 115
  references from corporate headings 173, 178
institutions *see* corporate bodies
International Standard Book Number
  see standard number area
International Standard Serial Number
  see standard number area
ISBN *see* standard number area
ISSN *see* standard number area

joint authorship *see* shared responsibility

language
  corporate headings 136
latest form of corporate names 137
levels of description 23, 202
librettists, collaborations with composers 60
local government *see* corporate bodies;
  government...; governments

main entries 44

manuscripts
  general material designation 14
maps
  special area 17
materials designation
  general 14
  specific 19
material (or type of publication)
  specific details area 2, 17
mayors 142
meetings *see* conferences
microforms
  general material designation 14
mixed authorship *see* mixed responsibility
mixed responsibility 52, 59
  added entries 88
  modifications of existing works 59, 60
  new works 60,63
modifications of existing works 60, 88
monographs *see* printed monographs
motion pictures
  general material designation 14
multimedia items
  general material designation 14
  physical description 28
multiple authorship 56
museums *see* corporate bodies
music
  general material designation 14
  special area 17
musical works 60, 62

name/title added entry headings
  analytical entries 191
name/title references 180
names, corporate *see* corporate headings
names, personal *see* personal names
national governments *see* corporate bodies;
    government...; governments
nobility, titles of *see* titles of nobility, honour,
    address, etc
nonprofit enterprises *see* corporate bodies
note(s) area 2, 21
numbers (*see also* standard number area)
  entry under, persons 115
numeric and/or alphabetic, chronological,
    or other designation of serials 9

objects
  general material designation 14
officials, government 142
omission, marks of 15
omissions
  from conference headings 139
  from personal names 106
  from statements of responsibility 15

other title information 12
pagination 19
  analytical entries 191
painters, as personal authors 45
paragraphing
  areas of description 8, 202
parallel titles 12
paraphrases 59
performers
  added entries 88
  as personal authors 45
  entry under 62, 206
performing groups *see* corporate bodies
periodicals *see* serials
personal authors
  entry under 45
  not named in item 51
  one only 48
  two or more *see* shared responsibility
personal names
  additions to 116
  choice 102
  compound names 112
  different names or forms of name 102, 104
  distinguishing between names which are
      the same 118
  entry element 111
  headings for 102
  omission of titles, etc, from statements of
      responsibility 15
  with prefixes 112
  without surname 106
phonogram dates *see* copyright dates
photocopies, description 23
photographers, as personal authors 45
phrases
  entry under, personal names 115
physical description area 2, 4, 19
place names *see* geographic names
place of publication, distribution, etc 4, 18
  two or more 10, 18
  unknown 204
playing time 19
postcards (*see also* graphic materials)
  worked example 199
posters (*see also* graphic materials) 29
predominant name
  corporate bodies 137
prefixes, names with
  entry element 112
prescribed sources of information *see* chief
    sources of information; sources of
    information
presidents 142
prime ministers 142
principal responsibility 53

printed monographs
  description 8
  entry
    changes of title 46
  worked examples 196, 197
proceedings (conferences) *see* conferences
programs, computer file designations 17
provinces
  added to corporate names 138
  added to place names 131
pseudonyms
  entry under 107
  references 173
publication dates 4, 18
publication, distribution, etc., area 2, 4, 18
publisher, distributor, etc 4, 18
  two or more 11, 18
  unknown 18
punctuation
  description (general) 1, 5, 8
  edition area 16
  physical description area 19
  publication, distribution, etc., area 5, 18
  serials 9
  series area 20
  title and statement of responsibility area 5, 15

qualifications of persons, omission
  from statements of responsibility 15

references *phase six*
regional governments *see* corporate bodies; government...; governments
related works 64
  added entries 88
  references 181
  see also adaptations; revisions; translations
religious bodies *see* corporate bodies
reprint dates 18
reproductions
  description 23
responsibility, statement of *see* statement of responsibility
revisers, added entries 88
revisions
  entry 59
  uniform titles not to be used 163
rewritings 59
Roman names
  entry under 115

sacred scriptures
  entry 45
  uniform titles 163, 166
scale

maps 17
scriptures *see* sacred scriptures
sculptors, as personal authors 45
'see also' references 175
'see' references 173
selections, from works by one person 45, 163, 167
serials
  description 9
  incomplete 209
  special area 9, 17
  worked example 201
series
  added entries 90
series area 2, 20
series statements 20
shared authorship 52
shared responsibility 52
single corporate body, works emanating from 48
single personal authorship 47
sound recordings
  entry under principal performer 62
  general material designation 14
  of musical or literary works 62
  worked example 206
sources of information 6
  access points 43
  edition area 7
  titles 12
sovereigns 142
special area, for cartographic materials, computer files, music and serials 9, 17
specific material designation 14, 19
standard number area 2, 8, 22
standardisation 1
statement of extent 19
statement of responsibility 2, 15
  relating to edition 16
states
  added to corporate names 138
  added to geographic names 131
subordinate corporate bodies 133, 140, 143
sub-titles 12
summary notes 21
supplementary items
  description 23
surnames 108
  compound *see* compound surnames
  entry element 112
  names containing, entry under 104
  names not containing 106
  nature uncertain 113
  with prefixes 112

terms of availability area 2, 22

three-dimensional objects
  physical description 19
title and statement of responsibility area 2,
  12
title entry 45
titles
  added entries 89
  capitalisation 12
  lack of 12
  references 180
  uniform titles 42, *phase five*
titles of nobility, honour, address, etc.
  added to personal names 116
  entry under 114
  in headings for personal names 106
titles of persons, omission from statement of
  responsibility 15
towns *see* cities
translations 60
translators, added entries 88

uncertain authorship *see* anonymous works
unhyphenated compound surnames 112
uniform titles 42, *phase five*
  added entries 170
  choice 164
  references 170, 180
  when to use 163
unknown authorship *see* anonymous works

unknown publisher 18
upper case letters
  headings 202
unnamed groups, works by 50

variant forms of corporate names 136
  references 178
variant languages of corporate names 136
  references 178
variant names
  corporate bodies 136
    references 178
  persons 107
    references 177
videorecordings
  general material designation 14
  physical description 19
volumes, number of 19

width of items 19
'with' notes 195
words or phrases
  entry under, persons 115
works, collective uniform title 167
works produced under editorial direction
  see collections
writers
  as personal authors 45
  collaborations with artists 60